SUPERIOR
CUSTOMER
SERVICE

*How to Keep Customers Racing
Back to Your Business—Time-Tested
Examples from Leading Companies*

By Dan W. Blacharski

SUPERIOR CUSTOMER SERVICE: How to Keep Customers
Racing Back to Your Business—Time-Tested Examples from Leading Companies

ISBN-13: 978-0-910627-52-8   ISBN-10: 0-910627-52-5

Library of Congress Cataloging-in-Publication Data
Blacharski, Dan, 1959-
   Superior customer service: how to keep customers racing back to your business--time-tested examples from leading companies / Dan W. Blacharski.
       p. cm.
   Includes bibliographical references and index.
   ISBN 13: 978 0 910627 52 8 (alk. paper)
   ISBN-10: 0-910627-52-5 (alk. paper)
   1. Customer services--Handbooks, manuals, etc. 2. Customer relations--Handbooks, manuals, etc.
I. Title.

HF5415.5.B523 2006
658.8'12--dc22

2006018645

ART DIRECTION, INTERIOR DESIGN: Meg Buchner • megadesn@mchsi.com
FRONT COVER & BOOK PRODUCTION DESIGN: Lisa Peterson, Michael Meister • info@6sense.net
EDITOR: Jackie Ness • jackie_ness@charter.net
EDITOR: Beth Williams • Creative Inklings LC • 412-683-2397 • beth@creativeinklings.org
www.creativeinklings.org
GLOSSARY COMPILED BY: Christina Mohammed

TABLE OF CONTENTS

CHAPTER 3: MULTIPLE CHANNELS OF CUSTOMER SERVICE   49

HIRING CUSTOMER SERVICE PEOPLE   65

CHAPTER 5: SWITCHING GEARS   81

CHAPTER 6: CUSTOMER SERVICE AS AN OPPORTUNITY TO CROSS-SELL AND UP-SELL   99

CHAPTER 7: GATHERING INFORMATION ABOUT YOUR CUSTOMERS   117

CHAPTER 8: CRUNCHING THE NUMBERS   129

CHAPTER 9: YOUR NEIGHBORHOOD CALL CENTER– NOW CONVENIENTLY LOCATED IN INDIA   135

CHAPTER 10: CUSTOMER SERVICE TECHNOLOGY 151

CHAPTER 11: CREATING CUSTOMER SERVICE IN AN ONLINE ENVIRONMENT   171

CHAPTER 12: CUSTOMER SERVICE STRATEGIES   189

FOREWORD

How often does customer service affect your business? Probably more often than you imagined…a person who has experienced poor customer service will most likely share their bad experience with an average of ten other people and cost your business money. Yet, how many businesses today focus on providing quality service that creates loyal customers?

Over the years, customer service has seemed to evaporate. Think back to when customer service was prevalent in our society. Back in the 1950's when gas station attendants would run out to your car to provide you with full service – filling your tank, checking under your hood and providing air to your tires when necessary. (Even if you do not recall those days, you do remember the image from the movie "Back to the Future.") Those days have been replaced with the convenience of do-it-yourself and limited access to human contact. You place your credit card into a machine; fill-up your own tank, and print out a receipt. However, what happens when technology doesn't work and you have to walk inside to give the clerk your credit card, or a receipt will not print? Convenience is taken awayand people become irritated. Now, your business is in the hands of how a customer service representative handles the situation that will determine if that customer returns another day.

So what can you do to improve your organization's customer service? *Superior Customer Service* provides a wealth of information from hiring individuals with the appropriate attitude, empowering staff and customers, choosing the appropriate types of technology, protecting customer information, increasing sales, and implementing best practices of customer service. It is a comprehensive book meticulously addressing the issues and decisions impacting customer satisfaction and outlining examples of companies whose customers continue to return time and again.

Providing superior service is the product of establishing an organization that has a core value of customer satisfaction and empowering every employee to honor that value. Too many organizations have silos or fiefdoms and the customer suffers due to an inability to care for the customer's needs. A previous employer once stated "If you aren't taking care of a customer, you darn well better be taking care of someone who is" and it has been a rule I have followed in my 15+ years of business.

Empowering your employees to take care of the customer will keep those customers raving about your service and always sprinting back for more.

Denise S. Starcher, MBA, SPHR

Denise Starcher is an innovative HR professional with expertise in organizational effectiveness, employee relations, compensation and benefits, and training and development. For the past 15 years, she has focused on enabling organizations to achieve sustained business growth while embracing change in the hospitality, healthcare, technology, and energy industries. She holds a MBA in General Management from Georgia State University, and a Bachelor of Science degree in Psychology from Centre College in Danville, Kentucky.

1 BASICS OF CUSTOMER SERVICE

E verybody's heard the expressions service with a smile, the customer is always right, and have a can-do attitude. We may have heard them so many times that they have become meaningless, but running a business today is more competitive than it has ever been, and providing the best customer service possible is often the only thing that can differentiate you from the competition.

Of course, there's a lot more to customer service than creating a lot of trite expressions and posting them on your break room bulletin board. Expressions like the customer is always right are all well and good, and they are important, but one must take a look at what's behind those expressions when creating a good customer service implementation. It involves creating a detailed strategy, implementing good customer service tactics, and, increasingly, using technology to help bring it all about. And in the spirit of modern-day management, we have even assigned this process a three-letter initialism: CRM (Customer Relationship Management).

But even before sophisticated business models and computer technology transformed the art of customer service into more of an exact science, customer service existed. When Mr. Macy started his first store, he made his customers feel welcome. When Mr. Ford made his first automobile, he did so with the intention of making his product accessible to the masses. Donut shop proprietors sometimes have a pleasant habit of putting "a little extra" into your box of a dozen, and modern department stores tend to go easy on you when you want to return something the next day but forgot your receipt.

THE CUSTOMER SERVICE GOLDEN RULE

Think of it as a customer service Golden Rule. How would you like to be treated when you go into a store? What kind of experience do you want when you shop online? Do you want to go through a lot of hassle, fill out a long form, and wait for a manager to come out and sign it, when all you want to do is exchange your 40-watt light bulbs for a pack of 60-watt bulbs?

Let's take a quick look at the history of this Golden Rule, a philosophy that has been handed down throughout the ages:

- "All things therefore that you want people to do to you, do thus to them." - *Christian*

- "Hurt not others in ways that you yourself would find hurtful." - *Buddhist*

- "That which you want for yourself, seek for mankind." - *Islam*

- "Do not impose on others what you do not desire others to impose upon you." - *Confucianism*

Customer service, in fact, has its roots in these simple and ancient philosophies. Regardless of the philosophy, these basic rules for living (and for the purpose of this book, for doing business) are based around the irrevocable fact that all people should have dignity, and there is a difference between right and wrong. We take into account how others feel and what they desire, and we try to do right by them when we are running a business. In doing so, we can feel better about ourselves as individuals, sleep the sleep of the righteous — and, ultimately, reap the rewards of our good deeds in terms of a successful and profitable business.

Although there has been customer service in one form or another for as long as there has been commerce, it has been varied in its approach. Today's era of e-commerce has created an environment where it is extraordinarily easy to compare prices, and even easier to switch suppliers. Buyers have easy access to conveniences like e-business exchanges, where they can see not only what you have to offer, but also what all your competitors — all around the world — have to offer as well, and at what price. Before this e-commerce model came into play, manufacturers, for example, frequently were at the mercy of their suppliers. They had to sort through massive paper parts catalogs and were often locked into long-term deals that gave suppliers, not their customers, the upper hand. It was, in many cases, difficult to switch, so customers tended to stick with the suppliers they had. This tendency didn't go unnoticed by suppliers. The supplier would not bend to accommodate the customer; rather, the customer had to bend to accommodate the conveniences of the supplier.

This is no longer the trend. As Forrester Research notes, "No longer can a company lay claim to a market segment and have free reign over the customers in that area." Customers and prospective customers have broader access to information today, and a global perspective on business, driven by the Internet, has changed the face of commerce—and as a consequence, customer service—forever. More companies have multiple distribution channels and global outlets, and even smaller companies can now compete on an international scale. These factors have made it difficult to set one's company apart from the pack. Differentiation has become blurred. Selling a product in this environment, especially online, is a great challenge when there are hundreds of other companies offering equivalent products at equivalent prices.

SETTING YOUR COMPANY APART

How can you, as a company, compete in this environment? There are more small fish in an increasingly large pond, all competing for the same piece of the action. The only solution is to find a way to set your company apart from the pack. Of course, you will strive to offer quality products at a reasonable price. But this no longer puts you ahead of the rest; it only puts you on an even playing level, even after you have already cut your prices to the bone. Besides competition from the global Internet, smaller companies, especially retailers, face price pressure from big-box retailers, further driving down prices and cutting margins. No, offering good products at the best prices won't set you apart; it will only keep you from sinking.

One of the only ways left to differentiate yourself from the increasing competition is to offer better customer service. Doing so requires a concentrated effort throughout the company, from top to bottom. Customer service is not just the responsibility of the service center or the call center. It's not limited to those who have first contact with the customer. Rather, it must come out of a comprehensive, integrated strategy that involves every single area of the company.

When customers buy a product from you, more often than not, it's a product that they could have gotten at any one of a hundred other places, and probably at the same price. There are three types of impressions that you can leave:

1. **The customers had a neutral experience, neither bad nor good.** Their product works to their expectations. You won't stand out in the customers' mind later on, and when they need another one, they will more than likely purchase it from whichever place is more convenient. There's no particular reason for them to come back to you. You have maybe a 50-50 chance of getting repeat business; less if there are more shops in your area that offer the same thing.

2. **The customers had a bad experience.** Perhaps the product works as expected and the price was reasonable, but a sales clerk ignored them or they had to wait in line too long. Your employees may not have been dressed professionally. Maybe the free coffee in your waiting room was stale and you were out of sugar. Unless you're a regulated monopoly and customers can't go elsewhere, you're out of luck here. No repeat business for you.

3. **The customers had a positive experience.** The product worked and was priced reasonably. They were served promptly by a friendly employee who answered all their questions and recommended a companion product that turned out to be a good buy as well. Your employee also recognized the customers as having been in before, greeted them by name, and gave them a free calendar. Next time, those customers will come back to you, even if somebody closer offers the same thing.

BUY-IN FROM MANAGEMENT

If you want your customer service to be the best, your customer service implementation, strategies, and CRM technology must start with a management buy-in. If the top brass doesn't actively support a customer service initiative, it won't succeed. There's a reason for this: customer service goes beyond the customer service department, and for this strategy to infiltrate the entire organization, it must start from the top and filter down.

That's not to say that the idea must come from the top brass, and more often than not, it doesn't. It's a matter of presenting the concept of improving customer service—and spending money on it—that must be presented effectively to the decision-makers to get their participation. Some customer service doesn't cost anything extra for the company: It doesn't cost anything extra for employees to keep a friendly attitude or to go out of their way to answer a question. Some customer service comes at only a very trivial expense; keeping fresh coffee in your waiting room is an example. But some customer service can be costly: Software systems designed to help your entire organization provide more efficient service to your customers can represent a major investment, and for this, there must be support at the highest levels.

The first thing you have to deal with in trying to get buy-in from executive staff is the attitude that customer service is a cost center. When something is seen as a cost center, it's often also seen as an area that can be cut — and is often the first one to get the axe when there's a budget crisis. "Need to trim the budget? No problem, let's lay off a few customer service guys."

That's the mindset that must be changed, and a good argument can be made that customer service is, in reality, much more than a cost center. It can also be a center for preserving existing revenue, and for generating new revenue as well. There are two areas your customer service department will make you money:

1. A good customer service center is an essential component in getting repeat business and referral business from happy customers.

2. A good customer service center will know the customers well enough to anticipate their needs. Cross-sell and up-sell, two very big revenue centers, come mainly out of the customer service center. Every contact with a customer is an opportunity for cross-sell and up-sell.

THINGS YOUR CUSTOMERS DON'T WANT TO HEAR

How many times have you, as a customer, been frustrated when trying to conduct a simple transaction that has been made unduly complicated by a beady-eyed underling bent on making your life miserable? Said underling goes "by the book." Strictly. At all times. And "the book" was written by people who never have to deal with customers directly, and it was written to accommodate back-end business processes that are, for the most part, obsolete anyway.

1. **"Your order is held up in the accounting department."** Customers don't want to hear that their business is being delayed by a bunch of bean-counters!

2. **"It takes a few days for that to go through processing."** This vague delay tactic implies that your customer's order is being delayed because it is on the bottom of a stack of papers on some underpaid clerk's desk. Why should processing take more than a few hours?

3. **"Oh, it looks like that didn't go through because you didn't fill out Form XG7-195234, Part 2-C(19)iii correctly. I'll send that back to you and you can re-submit."** Government agencies and regulated monopolies may get away with this, but you won't last long in business this way.

4. **"Sorry, the computer won't let me ring it up that way."** Computers are meant to make things more flexible. If the computer won't accommodate a customer, you need to change your computer programs, now.

5. **"My department doesn't handle that."** Customers don't care which department handles that; they just want it handled. Two words: integrated systems.

6. **"I don't know."** The worst response of all. Your company has computers, and information can and should be shared. There's no excuse for this at all.

Virtually all of these no-nos can be avoided with a more integrated approach to customer service. When every business process is created with an orientation toward serving the customer, none of these things will ever have to be said; this means every business process in every department in the entire company.

CUSTOMER-CENTRIC BUSINESS PROCESSES AND "THE EXTRA DONUT"

Implementing a strong customer service project involves changing every business process in the company to accommodate the customer. When a business process — any business process — is designed without thinking about the customer, the result is inevitably disastrous. IT is notorious for this. Computer programs, which ultimately serve customers or are used by customers to gain information about their accounts, are designed by IT, often for the convenience of IT. However, what makes perfectly logical sense to a computer programmer may be a convoluted mess to a customer. When designing a customer-facing program, IT must focus not only on how to make the program run efficiently on the back end, they must also design the program so it is friendly to the customer on the front end.

Part of creating customer-centric processes is the culture of extra effort. If you've ever visited New Orleans, you may be familiar with the word "lagniappe." Roughly translating to "a little bit extra," it's a culture of doing business that means putting forth extra effort, or giving customers more than they bargained for. It's the extra donut in the box.

When the sales clerk goes into the backroom and fishes out that pair of shoes that just suits you perfectly, instead of trying to sell you the ones that are "just okay," that's lagniappe. When tech support helps you fix your computer problem, even though it doesn't originate with their software, that's lagniappe. When the shop owner doesn't have what you want, and tells you which of his competitors do, that's lagniappe and then some.

THE CUSTOMER SERVICE MINDSET

In the coming chapters, I will talk a lot about strategies and tactics, and a lot about specific pieces of technology you can use to help create superior customer service. But aside from all the software, consultants, and three-letter initialisms, it all comes down to a frame of mind. There's a certain mindset involved in customer service, a culture, if you will, that must dominate the entire corporation, from the CEO down to the person who empties the wastebaskets at night.

Developing this mindset requires three things:

1. **Hiring "customer-oriented" employees**
   At some point or another, almost everyone in the company will have some type of interaction with a customer, even if that interaction is indirect. When a job candidate says to you, "I would prefer to work in the back office because I'm just not a 'people person,'" then

it's time to keep looking.

No department operates in a vacuum, and every single process, every single task that is completed, no matter how obscure or mundane, will affect the customer in some way.

2. **Creating a positive work environment**
Happy employees translate to happy customers. Creating and maintaining a positive work environment, free from office politics, hostility, and other nastiness, will help employees be in a service-oriented mood. And besides that, workplace hostility can lead to lawsuits!

3. **Providing ongoing customer service training**
Customer service training, first for all customer-facing employees but ultimately for everybody, is essential. Creating a culture of service requires constant vigilance, training, and education. In-service classes on customer service techniques, as well as classes on using customer-facing software applications and CRM tools effectively, will help you get the most out of what you have.

WHAT DOES YOUR COMPANY LOOK LIKE FROM THE OUTSIDE?

Part of developing the customer service mindset is looking the part. In some businesses, many employees will have actual contact with customers, and it makes sense to require them to look presentable. But what about the back office? Appearance there, too, makes a big difference, for two reasons: 1) There may be times when a customer or business partner must visit, or at least walk through, the business office, and 2) an overall professional appearance just helps to create a culture of service.

If you run a tattoo parlor that caters to bikers, your dress code is naturally going to be a lot different than if you run an upscale boutique in Manhattan. Let's consider the tattoo parlor for a moment. Your customers are going to feel more comfortable if they can feel a sense of kinship with the employees serving them. This is true for all businesses, not just the tattoo parlor. Let's imagine two scenarios:

1. Suppose for a moment that you're a member of the Hells Angels, and you park your Harley outside and stroll in to get your girlfriend's name tattooed on your arm. Inside the parlor you see a dozen or so neat cubicles, occupied by people in business suits. A guy in a black business suit and a narrow tie walks up to you, offers you Earl Grey tea in a china cup and instructs you to sit on a French antique sofa to wait. There are copies of *Forbes* and *The Wall Street Journal* for you to look at. "Easy listening" music is playing in the background. After a few moments, a secretary walks up to you and says, "Right this way, sir," and ushers you into one of the cubicles, where another guy in a suit hands you a leather-bound booklet that shows your various tattoo selections.

2. Suppose, again, that you are not a member of the Hells Angels, but rather an accountant who needs to take care of some banking business for a client. You drive up to the bank in your sensible, fuel-efficient car. You notice, when you get to the door, that adjacent to the "FDIC Insured" sign, there is a large poster of a heavy metal band. You walk inside and Aerosmith is playing on the radio at a

fairly loud volume, and a man in leathers with a beard like ZZ Top walks up to you, hands you a can of beer and says, "Take a load off, man," motioning toward what looks like the backseat from a '63 Chevy that has been pressed into service as a waiting room sofa. You wait, and leaf through the latest issue of Hot Rod magazine, until a young lady in a tank top and shorts comes out and says, "Come on back."

There's clearly something wrong with both of these pictures. A suit and tie doesn't always fit the situation, so you have to create a style of dress for your company that fits your culture. The guy in a business suit is probably going to make the tattoo parlor's customers nervous, as would the bearded, beer-drinking biker in the bank.

Dressing professionally, and dressing to suit the type of business you are in, will go a long way toward creating an environment where your employees feel like they are ready to go to work and your customers will feel at ease.

BASIC BUSINESS ETHICS

A company that adheres to good, basic rules of business ethics will be a company that offers good customer service. Many professional associations have Codes of Ethics for their members. Many larger companies and some smaller ones have a stated, written Code of Ethics by which they adhere. This code is often posted on the Web site and then forgotten, when it should be distributed to every employee throughout the company, and discussed freely at every company meeting.

Everyone should be aware of that Code, what's in it, and what it means for the business and the various processes that take place within it.

Customers clearly expect more today from companies than they ever have before. In the wake of corporate scandals, fiscal tomfoolery, and outright theft at the highest levels of corporate America, the buying public now seeks out information about how a company conducts its affairs and what it believes in. Having a good set of ethical ground rules that persist across the entire corporation at all levels is a good indicator to customers that they will be treated with respect. And that's just plain, good old-fashioned customer service.

The practice of developing the Code of Ethics in itself is a good exercise and should involve the broadest sector of the company possible. Creating this Code calls on a large cross-section of your organization to think about their business processes, how they approach their tasks, and how they will service their customers. It forces employees to think about and realize what their obligations are, both to the company and to the customer, and causes them to consider the best way to fulfill those obligations.

The Code itself is two things at once: It is inspirational and it outlines basic tenets and beliefs. More importantly, it outlines specific rules to which all employees must adhere. A Code of Ethics too often stops at the first part and falls short on the second. Look at the mission statements and "about us" pages of companies on the Internet, and you'll see a lot of so-called Codes that just fall short.

- "We adhere to the highest principles in our industry."

- "We are a Christian (or Muslim, or Buddhist, etc.) organization."

- "We believe in serving our customers."

These are all meaningless unless they are backed up with very specific details of how the company operates, how it treats its employees, and how it treats its customers.

UNRESOLVED PROBLEMS

When an employee is talking to a customer, that employee is a problem-solver. The first thing to do is to understand what the customer wants or needs. Sometimes it's easy: "I need to buy some black socks," the customer says. "They're right over here," you say. Simple.

But what if the customer has a more complicated request? A simple no is never an adequate response. Same with "I don't know." Before delivering one of those two dreaded utterances, try to find out more about the request. Get as many details as you can. Ask what the product will be used for if you're still not sure. "We don't have that, but we do have these over here," would be more acceptable. Or, as an alternative to the rude clerk who simply says "I don't know" and leaves it at that, say "I don't know, but I'll find out just what we can do for you." Never let customers walk away with an unresolved problem. If you simply can't deliver what they want, offer alternatives, and explain how those alternatives may suit them just as well.

Too often, we don't want to make exceptions. Exceptions are hard. They make us do extra work. We may have to manually enter something into the computer or ask somebody from another department to help. "The computer won't let me do that" is an excuse that has become too common, and we use that computer as an excuse to not service the customer. In fact, the computer is there to serve you, not the other way around. The computer will, in fact, let you do that, if you make it happen. And sometimes the only way to resolve a customer's problem is to make an exception. Create an organization that is built on flexibility, and empower your employees to make changes when needed so the result will be better service to the customer. Don't build hard-and-fast rules that can't be broken, and don't create business processes that are so narrow in focus that the customer seeking some slight variation will walk away not having been serviced.

CHAPTER 2

CREATING A CUSTOMER-CENTRIC CORPORATE CULTURE

C ompanies, like individuals, have distinct personalities. Think about the people you know and encounter in daily life. There are some people you enjoy being around and some people you would just as soon avoid. Some of your friends, co-workers, and acquaintances may be outgoing, friendly, and considerate. They may have overheard you say one day that you would like to have a pair of orange paisley socks but haven't been able to find any. One day they see a pair in an out-of-the-way boutique. They think of you, buy the socks, and then go out of their way to give them to you the next day. Why? Because they're thoughtful. They knew you wanted those socks, and they got some joy out of solving a problem for you.

On the other hand, some people may be all business, all the time. When you go to lunch, they divide the bill down to the penny and figure the tip with a calculator. Or they may be pushy, always trying to get you to buy into some fantastic multi-level marketing deal they're involved in, and they may cling to routines unnecessarily to the point of being compulsive.

The funny thing is when a person sticks to the same routine, day in and day out, even after the reason for that routine has long been forgotten. They are said to be obsessive-compulsive and are given drugs. When a company does the same thing, it is praised by analysts and bean-counters for being "conservative" and "business-like."

What do you want your company's personality to be like? From a customer service perspective, your company's personality should be one that makes people want to interact with it.

THE CORPORATE CULTURE AND CUSTOMER SERVICE

What does the corporate culture have to do with customer service? Plenty. Your company's personality will reflect through every single person in it, and, ultimately, it will reflect in how your product is created, whether it is created with the customer in mind, and how those employees that have contact with customers will represent you.

MISSION STATEMENT

Almost every company has a mission statement. Even if it's not written out, you do have a mission with your company, and more often than not, your stated mission is the starting point of your company's service culture. Naturally, the unwritten element of that mission is that you wish to make a profit. But the way that comes about is what makes up the mission statement.

This isn't the place to make statements about your mission to make buckets full of money for you and your stockholders. "Delivering fair value and a good return to stockholders," while necessary, is a statement that does not belong in the mission statement. Save the money-making hype for the annual report.

Keep in mind that your mission statement is going to be placed on your Web site for the public to see. It is, therefore, part strategy and part public relations, and it should be written with that in mind. The mission statement is, and should be, all about the customer. It should reflect the following, and should be created using positive statements:

- Your commitment to customers.

- Your desire to deliver good value to customers.

- Your belief in delivering the best service possible.

But don't just leave it at the fuzzy feel-good stage. It should also include some specifics about how you deliver the above; for example, showing your commitment to some or all of the following:

- Providing quality goods at the best prices.

- Providing training and resources to your support staff to enable them to deliver quality service.

- Use of technology to enhance the customer experience.

- Utilize the most modern manufacturing techniques to produce the best product possible.

Once you have your magnificent mission statement completed,

what do you do with it? You'll post it on your Web site and hand it to your PR people to include in your press material, of course. But besides that, the mission statement should serve as an actual working document that has a purpose behind it.

From that statement, every single other business process flows. Let's take "use of technology to enhance the customer experience" as an example. This point should be posted on the computer screen of every single member of your IT department. If any of your customer service agents says, at any time, "No, the computer won't let me do that," then you have failed in your mission. First of all, the computer should let them do that, and if it's not possible for the computer to do whatever "that" is, then there should be a manual way to override it and accomplish the task. Computers are not meant to be inflexible. Computers become inflexible when the IT staff that programs them strays from the mission and forgets that what they are doing is meant to service the customer.

YOUR CORPORATE VALUES

While the mission statement reflects what you, as a company, specifically intend to do and provide from a customer service perspective, a "value statement" is allowed to be a little less specific. This merely reflects your values as a company (again, from a customer service perspective).

Your corporate culture reflects your values as a company, and, ultimately, what is most important to a company will affect how your customers see you. A good starting point to use when defining your corporate culture is to identify what is important to you. Obviously, making money is important, but go beyond that. Start by asking yourself the following questions:

1. How do you want your customers to see you?

2. If you were the customer and not the business executive, what would you like to change about your company?

3. Name the thing about your company you are most proud of.

4. Do you go out of your way to provide service to a customer?

5. How flexible are you in your day-to-day business policies?

The insurance industry is one that, above all others, revolves around customer service. For example, if customers buy car insurance but never have an accident, they never get a chance to actually use the product they are paying for. Their only chance to see value from all that money they pay every month is in how good the insurance company, or its agents, treats them. Did the agent go out of his or her way to make sure everything is taken care of? Did the agent find the customer the best rates possible and apply all available discounts? Did the agent generally make the customer feel welcome? Insurance companies live and die on customer service. Surly agents, inconvenient hours, long hold times on the phone, inflexible payment methods, and a confusing and intimidating claims process will put an insurance company out of business before they know it.

Progressive Casualty Insurance Company is one company

that knows how to take care of their customers. Their internal corporate culture is reflected in their statement of values, and it all revolves around serving the customer. The following is Progressive's value statement—take a detailed look at it, and realize that this company's corporate culture is all about service.

Our Values

Governing our vision, decisions and behavior are our core values—pragmatic statements of what works best for us in the real world.

Integrity

We revere honesty. We adhere to the highest ethical standards, provide timely, accurate and complete financial reporting, encourage disclosing bad news and welcome disagreement.

Golden Rule

We respect all people, value the differences among them and deal with them in the way we want to be dealt with. This requires us to know ourselves and to try to understand others.

Objectives

We strive to communicate clearly Progressive's ambitious objectives and our people's personal and team objectives. We evaluate performance against all these objectives.

Excellence

We strive constantly to improve in order to meet and exceed the highest expectations of our customers, shareholders and people. We teach and encourage our people to improve performance and to reduce the costs of what they do for customers. We base their rewards on results and promotion on ability.

Profit

The opportunity to earn a profit is how the competitive free-enterprise system motivates investment to enhance human health and happiness. Expanding profits reflect our customers' and claimants' increasingly positive view of Progressive.

Reprinted with permission of Progressive Casualty Insurance Company.

CREATING A SERVICE-ORIENTED CULTURE

A service culture isn't something that just happens, or something you can mandate by writing a memo. Similarly, you may create a mission statement or vision statement that claims something to the effect of "We strive to always do our best to put the customer first," but that statement, without specific policy items to back it up and enforcement of those policy items, are useless—and are little more than feel-good claptrap.

Creating a service culture in your company is a long and complicated process and it involves several steps. And once you've created it, you have to maintain it, every single day. Here are the steps:

- Know your customer.

- Create a customer service strategy.

- Hire the right people.

- Customer service training.

- Implement standards and record metrics.

- Positive reinforcement.

- Start at the top.

- Keep your employees happy.

We'll discuss each one in the following sections.

KNOW YOUR CUSTOMER

Before you can provide good customer service, you have to know your customer. This involves two things: 1) understanding who they are, and 2) understanding what they want. The first part of this is easy: Simply noticing who walks in the front door and taking note of who buys and who doesn't will tell you who they are. Those who have been in business for a while will know their main demographic, whether it's women between 20 and 35, men over 40, married or single, fashionable or down-to-earth. If your business is online, this is even easier, and we'll discuss some technological ways of knowing your customers better in Chapter 10.

Understanding what customers want is another matter entirely, but knowing what they want is what makes a business successful. The first thing to do is provide an easy conduit for your customer-facing employees to talk to you, and the second thing to do is to listen to them. If you run a retail shop, for example, nobody in the company will know better what customers want than the sales clerks. If you're a large retail outfit, you probably hire a staff of college-educated and highly paid buyers, most of whom wear trendy clothes and enjoy the status of their position but never really talk to customers, instead pretending to know enough to set fashions on their own. In reality, your sales clerks, who may have only graduated high school and have no status to speak of, would make better buyers. Listen to what they have to say.

One way to both know who your customers are and what they want is to take a customer feedback survey. It's a simple technique that doesn't require a lot of technology. You can divide your customers into potential accounts, light-volume accounts, and heavy-volume accounts, and in so doing, you can gain a lot of valuable insight into what makes people buy more and what makes them buy less.

A focus group is another excellent method, and something customers and other people often look forward to participating in. Make your focus group a fun event and provide some sort of reward, such as a free dinner or a coupon for half off their next purchase. Recruit several customers from a good cross-section of your customer base, and bring them all together in a comfortable venue, perhaps a restaurant's banquet room. Give your customers some general direction as to what you want them to discuss, but make the whole event as open and free-wheeling as possible. Be quiet and take lots of notes. You'll be surprised as to what sorts of ideas come up.

CREATE A CUSTOMER SERVICE STRATEGY

You have created a mission statement and a vision statement, and perhaps several other statements. You've taken steps to understand who your customers are and what they want, and now you must create a coherent strategy for customer service.

The mission statement you created is the foundation of your strategy, but don't make the mistake of thinking that the mission statement is your strategy in its entirety. The mission statement is general; your strategy is specific. Like your mission statement, your strategy should be written, but unlike your mission statement, it need not be made public on your Web site. Your customer service strategy should, nonetheless, be an important part of every single business process you have.

Here is where you create another focus group, only this time, it's made up of staff members from throughout your company. It should include executives, middle management, and front-line workers. It should include at least one representative from every department, whether that department interacts directly with customers or not.

This is where you create a list of specific policies, action items, and procedures designed to provide the best customer service. You might be surprised at the ideas that come up. And because you've included a cross-section of your staff from all levels, you might discover that your company has been lacking in certain areas. All the front-line employees know it, but nothing has ever been done about it. It happens all the time. All the staff knows that a certain business process disservices customers, but you, the business owner or executive, have been blissfully unaware of this fact for years because nobody ever dared to tell you.

As part of this process, you may wish to reevaluate some or all of your business processes. Ask all department heads to list their various business processes, and then ask this question: Does this process enhance or detract from customer service?

Here's an example: XYZ Company has several items in stock but will take special orders. When a customer makes a request for a special order, the employee must call over a supervisor, who must fill out a form and sign off on it. On many occasions, customers have had to wait several minutes for the supervisor. Is it really necessary to bring the supervisor over? Probably not. Empower your front-line employees! They probably already have the knowledge they need to take the special orders, and if they don't, give it to them. Let them handle it themselves.

HIRE THE RIGHT PEOPLE

One can never talk too much about hiring, and your hiring strategy will have a big effect on your customer service culture. Of course, you must hire people who have the right skill sets and educational backgrounds. But besides that, there is something a little fuzzier that your hiring managers must pin down when making decisions, and that is each candidate's customer service attitude. The customer service focus of candidates is perhaps even more important than their existing skills. Skills can be taught later; attitudes are hard to change.

In evaluating attitude, there are a few legal caveats, and it may be a good idea to run your interview questions list by your legal department ahead of time. You can't, for example, take it upon yourself to decide that a religious person would provide better service and ask job candidates whether they attend church. You can't decide you'd rather have married people, because they would be more settled, and ask questions about marital status. And you can't ask if they have kids, because you believe that someone without kids would be able to devote more energy to your company. In reality, these things matter very little, anyway.

You can, however, take special notice of the job candidate's attitude and demeanor during the interview, and you can ask them pointed questions about what they would do in various customer service situations. Create a list of very open-ended questions designed to allow candidates to talk. Ask the question, then be quiet and listen.

Many prominent companies use a battery of tests as part of the hiring process. Although, in the end, it's still a judgment call, these tests can help you determine who will be best suited for your company from a customer service perspective. Skills testing is common in most industries and is an excellent way to find out whether a candidate can do the job in question. Some companies even administer an IQ test in addition to that. But, perhaps, the most important test is the personality test. These are standardized tests that don't necessarily even relate to the specifics of your industry; rather, they measure a candidate's "people" abilities. They will tell you whether candidates will be a good co-worker and whether they will be good at working with customers. These tests are surprisingly accurate and very effective as a tool used in the hiring process.

CUSTOMER SERVICE TRAINING

Some companies take their new employees and throw them right into the fray, without taking time to explain the ropes. Sure, the new employee has skills, but he doesn't yet know how you do things there and doesn't understand what your goals are. There are two things you have to do to here: 1) an initial employee orientation, and 2) ongoing customer service training.

The initial orientation is more than just taking them around for an introduction and showing them where the break room is and how the coffee pot works. This is where the employees get to understand your company mission, your vision, and your strategies. This is where all new employees come to understand that you have a focus on customer service, and that it will be part of their job to reflect that focus in everything they do.

"But that should be understood," you say. Not necessarily. Employees come to you from all over. They may have come from a company that had different strategies and treated their customers in a far different manner than you. They may have come from a company that has inflexible policies and will not go out of their way to satisfy a customer who wants something out of the ordinary. Your policies are more flexible, and you want your people to be willing to satisfy those customers who want something a little different. Employees who came from the inflexible environment may think it normal to tell a customer,

"Sorry, can't do that." When, in reality, you would prefer that they say "We don't have that now, but let me see if the guys in the shop can fix that up for you."

You will naturally give your new employees copies of your corporate policy manuals, but don't let the orientation begin and end with this handoff. Take the time to discuss the policies in detail, and give specific examples of how each of these policies work.

IMPLEMENT STANDARDS AND RECORD METRICS

A company that lives and dies by the numbers is one that won't be in business for too long. But having said that, those numbers will be a very important part of your customer service strategy. You will, as part of your strategy, implement a series of customer service standards. Every employee should understand these standards. And what's more, you need to keep track of how well those standards are implemented.

As an example, fast-food restaurants have a hard focus on standards, and their very success depends on adhering to standards of speedy service. They may say, for example, that every drive-through customer must receive his or her food within 60 seconds. Many fast-food restaurants keep careful track of this goal, and a clock will start ticking the moment an order has been taken. The counter employee will hit the timer again after the food has been delivered. This is part of the ongoing process, every single time, for every single customer. Reports are created to show how well that goal is being met, and whether it is being met only at certain times. They will also know which employees are meeting or exceeding the time goal and which ones are falling behind.

POSITIVE REINFORCEMENT

Positive reinforcement is everything in managing employees. The paycheck isn't enough by itself. It's the little extras, the "attaboys" and the pats on the back that make employees feel more like part of a team. And when they feel like they're on a team, they're going to take it upon themselves to represent that team to the best of their ability — that means delivering better customer service. Additionally, a little positive reinforcement goes a long way toward reducing employee churn. In most industries, the process of hiring and training a new employee is expensive, and customers often resent the constant changing of faces. The extra reinforcement will pay off in terms of a better customer service orientation and happier customers who spend more money.

Positive reinforcement comes in all sizes. Financial bonuses are always welcome, and many companies provide bonuses based on either individual performance, company-wide performance, or both.

Social bonuses are also instrumental in creating a "team" environment. This includes occasional hosted dinner parties for the entire company, or even less formal events where managers take their departments out for a long lunch (on the company dime, of course).

START AT THE TOP

If you want to create a service-oriented corporate culture, it has to start at the top. Management's own personal attitude toward customers is going to reflect throughout the rest of the company, regardless of any company policy or directives. It just won't work to tell employees to take good care of customers when you don't have a service attitude yourself. If you're a manager, executive, or proprietor, here are some simple things you can do to improve your company's customer service attitude:

- **Spend a little time every week working directly with customers.** Get on those front lines and take orders for an hour or two. Put on the paper hat and stand behind the counter. Man the phones while the receptionist takes lunch. Sure, you have other things to do, but even just a token effort will go a long way in setting an example and showing your staff (and your customers) that you really do have a service-oriented attitude.

- **Solicit regular feedback from the staff that has the most contact with the customer.** Ask them what's working, what's not, and what should be changed. Too often, processes are left in place simply because that's the way it's always been done, even though it disservices the customers and may cause them confusion or extra work.

- **You need to see for yourself what the customer experience is like.** If it's possible to play the role of customer, and go into your own shop and place an order without being recognized as the boss, do so. If not, hire a secret shopper to do it for you.

KEEP YOUR EMPLOYEES HAPPY

He's overworked, sometimes pulling double shifts. Sometimes he has to give up part of his lunch hour because things get backed up. He doesn't make as much money working for you as he could working for somebody else. He gets two weeks' paid vacation but can't take it when he wants to because your nephew, who works in the same department, wants to take his vacation at the same time. You snarled at him when he came in ten minutes late the day the bus broke down, and you yelled at him when he didn't get the extra work done that you assigned to him. When he broke the dress code and wore a paisley tie to work one day, you made him go home and change, and docked his pay for the time it took to do it.

You've created a time bomb.

He's dissatisfied and angry; he's mad at you and thinks you're a nitwit. He is intimidated by you and hates every minute of his job. What's going to happen here? He's going to take it out on your customers. His dissatisfaction is going to be reflected in his work and in his interactions with your customers, and you can't blame him. You probably have a high staff turnover, and this, too, affects your customers in a negative way. Customers like familiarity, and they like dealing with the same people over and over again.

Service Example

Let's take a group of guys who have been going to their favorite local pizza restaurant every Tuesday at noon for the last twenty-five years. It's not a big chain restaurant; it's a family-owned shop. When one of the gang leaves town for a few months and then returns, the bartender remembers where he went and asks "How was your trip?" And what's more, the waitress behind the counter always remembers your order before you even have a chance to say it. She's been there for years and always gives you the two-dollar discount even though you never have the coupon with you. Now here's a business that obviously has happy employees who are treated well.

Creating happy employees (that, in turn, create happy, regular, paying customers) is the job of management. Here are some simple things you can do:

- Make sure everybody knows when a customer calls or writes to praise an employee's good service.

- When everyone has to work late, make it pleasant. Let the neckties come off, and order pizza for everyone.

- Empower your employees with the ability to bend the rules and make decisions on their own, when it benefits the customer.

- Reward for meeting milestones. For example: When your company hits a million dollars a month in volume (or whichever amount is realistic), host a party for employees and their spouses.

- Implement a feedback system to allow employees at all levels to make suggestions—and then listen to those suggestions.

CharterAuction

CharterAuction CEO Nate McKelvey attributes his company's strong growth to its concierge department and the high level of personalized customer service the company delivers. CharterAuction, which offers private jet charter services, is truly a service-oriented company. While a commercial airliner may serve up standard fare in the form of uninspiring meals (if you get any at all), bags of pretzels, and seats that just aren't practical for normal-sized people, CharterAuction's blue-ribbon catering service determines each client's preferences on more than 50 items prior to a trip.

"Everyone in the company, including myself, spends virtually all of our time and energy on service-related issues," says Nate. And CharterAuction has made excellent use of technology in the delivery of customer service, with their own proprietary technology platform designed to track and service every customer. "CharterAuction tracks the progress throughout their entire experience with us. All departments access the system including sales/marketing, fulfillment, concierge, and accounting. Customers have access to all of the information pertaining to their flight status, and vendors access the system to make sure orders are filled correctly." CharterAuction consultants and concierge representatives are on call 24 hours a day to accept any request from customers, via e-mail, phone, or walk-in.

The company has developed extensive training procedures, manuals, and systems to help make sure that customer service personnel are knowledgeable and capable of servicing clients. "Our system and training programs are very thorough, which gives us the ability to hire people who may not have industry knowledge."

"Personalized service sets us apart from the other competitors," said Nate. "Our technology removes many of the mundane tasks most of our competitors face. This gives our people the time to interact on a personal basis with our clients. We take note of passengers on each flight, catering preferences and background of each customer. The information is then attached to the client's record in our system for future reference and company-wide access."

Customer feedback is very important at CharterAuction. Nate personally requests feedback after every trip, rating everything from the aircraft selection process to the concierge department, aircraft, crew, and catering. Customers receive a personal touch from every level. Nate says, "Nothing works as well as personal on-site visits with clients, especially when there is a customer service issue." CharterAuction has gained the trust and respect of its clients also by transparently displaying detailed information about each jet operator for the customer's trip, including safety rating, pictures of the plane, crew experience, and price. "Customer trust is the most important factor to retain long-term relationships."

Sooner or later, though, everybody gets a dissatisfied client, and when that rare occasion occurs, Nate turns a negative into a positive. "When a customer has a poor experience," he says, "I get involved and respond directly to the customer feedback survey. I fully investigate the issue, including a review of our internal log files and notes for the trip, a call to the vendor, and a meeting with the key contact person for the customer. I then write a detailed response and follow up with a phone call." And Nate goes the extra mile by making himself accessible. "All clients have my personal 24-hour contact information," he says. "If there is a problem, I want the client to have access to me."

CHAPTER 3

MULTIPLE CHANNELS OF CUSTOMER SERVICE

I f you want to provide good customer service—and we'll assume that you do—one of the first things you have to do is make your company accessible. While most companies make every effort to make it easy for customers to place orders and shop, fewer companies go out of their way to make it easy for people to complain. Yet, this is precisely what you must do.

Some common mistakes that companies, both large and small, make in terms of accessibility include the blind Web site. This involves creating an otherwise wonderful and informative Web site, but there is no contact information listed, no feedback mechanism, and no way to ask a question. The creators of such a site imagine that they have provided everything that the customer could possibly want to know, and there's either no need to provide a response mechanism, or they don't want to take the time. Either way, it's a mistake. And that response mechanism must be complete. You must provide an e-mail address for customer service contacts, or at least a feedback form, and you must also provide information about your physical location. As much as you don't want to spend money on staffing the phones, you must also include a phone number.

Some utility companies, for example, have had the audacity to eliminate local customer walk-in payment centers, leaving customers to make their payments at small, independent contractors housed in gas stations and corner groceries that will charge you a dollar for the privilege of taking your money. This is customer service at its worst. Very few non-monopoly companies could get away with charging people to make payments!

ALIGN YOUR PROCESSES WITH CUSTOMER NEEDS

According to a recent Iinternational Data Corporation (IDC) study, virtually all sales and marketing people believe that aligning marketing efforts and sales initiatives with customer needs is important. However, the same study showed that sales and marketing people aren't measuring up to their own expectations, with only 66 percent of respondents stating that they are in alignment.

So where is the misalignment? All over the map. The IDC study showed that some respondents said they were weak in the awareness and consideration phases of the buy cycle, when customers are still in the "looking around" phase; while others are more misaligned in the later stage. Misalignment in the early stage means losing out on a potential customer, and misalignment in the later stage means lower customer retention. Either way, it's lost money. It's clear that many vendors do not have the adequate understanding of their customers and often have not established the level of contact they require and the feedback mechanisms that are essential to develop customer relationships.

EQUAL TIME

The Internet has made it possible for us to offer many new and different means of customer contact. Customers can now interact with your call center via e-mail, real-time online chat, instant messaging, fax-back, online form, or even PC-to-voice connection. But one thing is sometimes forgotten in the midst of all these technological mechanisms: Not every customer has a computer, and even many of those who do, don't want to use it to talk to you.

It is therefore vitally important to keep open multiple channels of customer contact so that the customers may receive service through whichever means is most convenient to them.

It is true that some methods of customer contact are less expensive than others, and it is tempting to restrict your customer contact to things like e-mail, while discouraging telephone contact or actual one-on-one, face-to-face contact. This, of course, is a big mistake, and in the long run will cost you more than you save. According to a Jupiter Research study, many companies are far too slow in responding to online requests for information.

The best customer service center will not only offer multiple channels of customer contact but will also make each one equally responsive. A very common mistake is to offer customers the opportunity to communicate via e-mail but then require them to wait two or three days for a response—while customers who call in over the phone can get a response within ten or twenty minutes. Each method should get equal treatment. Consider offering your customers at least three or four of the following options to get service:

- Walk-in

- Telephone contact

- Live Internet chat

- E-mail

- Fax-back for information

- Click for call-back

Above all, integrate your customer service. Every customer service area should have access to precisely the same information and should be able to deliver the same speedy response. Forrester Research points out the potential for failure here: "Large companies risk poor customer service daily due to the grab bag of independent applications they use to support their customers. While this problem has existed for years, it will soon end as the Web becomes an ever-stronger force and high-quality self-service becomes a competitive differentiator."

For more information about some of the technological solutions above, see Chapter 10, "Customer Service Technology." Briefly, live Internet chat lets your customers contact you via a private internet-messaging window. "Click for call-back" is a simple system that places an icon on your Web site, which customers can click, and then enter their phone number into a dialog box.

This information is immediately sent to your call center so the customer can receive a call back on a timely basis.

E-SERVICE

The Internet has become a prominent means of providing customer service, and more customers today are seeking information online. As the Internet becomes more sophisticated, more pervasive, and more information-rich, your customers will come to expect much more of their online interaction with you. If you want to stay competitive, you'll have to comply. As discussed above, this doesn't mean replacing your entire customer service department with a purely online customer response mechanism. It does mean that you must offer a sophisticated and responsive online customer response mechanism.

There may be a few Luddites still out there who will say that old-fashioned customer service, offered by a live person, is always best and always preferred. But, that's just not so. Many customers today prefer the convenience of online interaction, and this should always be offered as an option and an alternative to live contact.

One of the most common types of e-service to put up is the common Frequently Asked Questions (FAQ) page on your Web site. The old 80/20 rule applies: 80 percent of your customer requests can usually be answered with 20 percent of your most common responses. To be sure, many requests will be non-standard and will have to be handled elsewhere, but both you and your customer can save time and money by posting answers to common questions in this easy format.

UNIFIED INFORMATION

In some cases, customer service information is driven by individual departments tasked with specific areas of customer service. If customers have a question about their account, the accounting department may be the one to handle the request. If it's a request for customization, they may be sent to manufacturing; if they want to place a new order, they may be sent to the sales department. Each different department may have different silos of customer information that sit behind customer processes that are executed separately and individually.

Having multiple customer processes that are not unified, each one in a separate department being driven by separate databases of information, is lost money. The company that takes this approach will lack the synergies that can be gained from unifying the processes and information. Cross-sell and up-sell is an obvious example. While the sales department may be in tune with the need to cross-sell, other departments may not have access to the same information. The manufacturing department won't necessarily know that the customer purchased product "A" last month and would benefit by acquiring the complementary product "B." The key to success in this regard is to make sure that each department that has contact with the customer is tapping into the same database and using the same applications.

Every employee that has any contact with the customer, whether direct or indirect, should be given a 360 degree view of that customer. Doing so will ensure that no opportunities for cross-sell and up-sell get lost and that all relevant customer information is available at all times, by all personnel, to better service the customer.

There are dozens of different ways your customers may choose to contact you. To make your customer service the most effective, make each method equal, give each the same attention, and provide prompt responses regardless of the method of communication. Integration is the vital glue that holds it all together. If a customer makes a phone call and connects to your call center, your call center staffers should be able to easily look on their computer screen and see their entire history of interaction. They should be able to tell at a glance that they discussed a shipping issue with the fulfillment area; they arranged for credit with your credit department; they placed a special order with sales; and they made adjustments to that order with the manufacturing department. Furthermore, your staffer should be able to see all of that on a single screen, from a single application.

OFFICE POLITICS AND DEPARTMENTAL FIEFDOMS

Corporate dynamics are a curious thing. There's no question that people enjoy the power they are able to acquire over the course of their tour of employment.

In the corporations of old, the approach to management was to do as much as possible in-house, to grow a huge organization with multiple divisions and departments, and to have an endless supply of middle managers to oversee each business process. And granted, before computer technology lent a bit of unification and simplicity to management, much of this was probably necessary. At one time, it took an entire roomful of clerks to do what one part-timer with an electronic spreadsheet can do today.

In those days, all those middle managers were like watchdogs over their individual departments and processes. They were jealous of their information and tended to keep things secret. Their departmental files stayed in their departments. There was an enormous amount of duplication going on.

The modern methods of management revolve around a lean approach. The modern corporation runs on information, and because we have computers and databases, it's no longer necessary for each department to maintain their own redundant information.

Nonetheless, even though it is absolutely unnecessary and is counterproductive, it still happens. Department heads create their own little fiefdoms and build their own private silos of information. That information is kept within the department, even though it could benefit the rest of the corporation. Why? Simply because of human nature. We enjoy having power. Sometimes we feel that in maintaining absolute control over processes and information, we will gain more power.

In fact, the opposite is true. Information equals power in today's corporate environment, but it's not about who has the most; it's about sharing it. A corporation with individual centers of power, and individual islands of information, is, in fact, not a powerful corporation at all. The most powerful corporation will be the one that provides a more universal base of access to customer data to all who need it.

TEAMWORK

A basic element of good customer service is teamwork. It's a simple concept, it doesn't necessarily require a lot of technology behind it, and it's something that many companies don't pay enough attention to.

Promoting teamwork is another one of those things that creates a lot of overused expressions. While it's true that there is no "I" in "team," creating a spirit of teamwork involves a lot more than putting up slogans on the walls.

It's not necessarily a hiring issue, either. Your hiring managers may say "We want to hire team players" until they're blue in the face, but it will make little difference. Team players are made after the fact. People generally come to a job for personal reasons — they want to make more money, they want a greater challenge, or they want more responsibility. In reality, very few people take a job because they want to be part of a team. That's just something people put on their résumés to impress the boss.

And it's as it should be. A job is not an altruistic activity. But, after you bring on the best people you can find, that's the time to build a team. Once you have a group of team players, your customers will be serviced appropriately. An employee who is a team player will go out of his or her way to give a customer service, even if it means going outside of the job description or bringing in other personnel to help solve the customer's problem. Here are a few points on creating a team:

Promote Information Sharing

A team cannot exist if employees do not have access to the information they need to do their jobs. Prevent "information hoarding" by creating a framework in which everyone who requires information has easy access to it. Centralize customer databases and avoid circumstances where individual departments maintain vital customer information in databases that cannot be accessed from outside of their area.

Use Communication Technology

Make it easy for employees to communicate, whether they are across the office or on the other side of the world. Proprietary instant-messaging platforms make an excellent way for employees to communicate, as well as e-mail, conferencing software, and VoIP (voice-over Internet protocol) services that make it possible to easily and cheaply call other employees or partners anywhere in the world at low cost.

No Rigid Job Descriptions

"That's not my job" is the mantra of the lazy and is a statement that should never be uttered in a company striving for good customer service. The job of each individual in the organization is to serve the customer to the best of his or her ability. By enforcing rigid job descriptions, you prevent employees from venturing out of the standard protocol to solve a customer's problem. If employees must do something out of the norm, or outside of their regular job description, for the benefit of a customer, then it should be acceptable, even expected for them to do so.

Empower Employees

The best customer service will be provided by a flexible organization staffed by people who are knowledgeable about every process in your company, capable of making decisions on their own, and capable of crafting creative solutions for a customer. Sometimes the best customer service employee is the one who doesn't go by the book.

A WORD ABOUT SECURITY

A company must share information to survive. Remaining competitive depends on it, and information sharing is at the very heart of good customer service.

But there is a framework of legislation, and just plain common sense, when it comes to sharing. Certain types of customer data, such as account numbers, passwords, credit card numbers, and other financial data, must, of course, be safeguarded to prevent things like identity theft.

While your customers will expect the people they talk to within your company to know who they are, what they want, and how to solve their problem, they will also expect their privacy to be respected. It is, therefore, somewhat of a delicate balancing act to share the information that must be shared in order to provide excellent customer service, while at the same time safeguarding the information that must be kept private in order to comply with the law.

Security technology that enables secure authorization and authentication is an essential part of corporate life. You must create an access policy that sets out ahead of time precisely which individuals and which departments need access to which pieces of information in order to better do their jobs or to better serve the customer. If the need is not there, then access should be denied. For example: It would be useful, indeed, for the sales staff to have easy access to a record of what each customer has ordered in the past, but it's probably not necessary for the sales staff to have access to the customer's private credit information. Salespeople would, of course, need to know, generally, the status of the customer's credit so as to allow or disallow a purchase to be made. For example, the salesperson should be able to say to customers whether their credit status would or would not allow them to make a certain purchase. The manufacturing department, on the other hand, may not have any need to know about a customer's credit status, since the order has already been made and approved.

Credit card information is obviously one of the biggest concerns, and this must be watched over with an iron fist.

A SUMMARY OF INFORMATION PRIVACY REGULATIONS

CISP (VISA Cardholder Information Security Program)

This is a program created by VISA USA that protects cardholder information, regardless of where it resides. It requires you, as a merchant or service provider, to maintain a certain standard of information security. It involves adhering to a set of best practices as well as implementing information technology solutions to safeguard this customer data. Part of this involves restricting the physical access to cardholder information, storing it only when necessary, not using default configurations, and purging obsolete data frequently. Recommended technology includes firewalls, antivirus software, and strong authentication.

Gramm-Leach-Bliley Act

This piece of federal legislation requires all financial institutions to guarantee that customer records and information is confidential and secure. Guidelines have been created by the U.S. Department of Treasury regarding these safeguards, designed to protect the security, confidentiality, and integrity of customer information.

HIPAA (Health Insurance and Portability Accountability Act)

Passed by Congress to improve the effectiveness of the health care system, HIPAA is a far-reaching piece of legislation that addresses many different areas of health care. Part of HIPAA was designed to reduce the incidence of fraud and to protect the privacy of patient information. The automation of health care has brought many efficiencies, but when patient information is transferred between computers, there is an inherent security risk. Health care providers of all types must secure patient records through technological means.

Sarbanes-Oxley Act

Section 404 of Sarbanes-Oxley requires the officers of publicly held companies to certify that their internal controls are effective as they relate to the accuracy of financial information.

California Information Practice Act

If your company maintains any personal or financial information about a California resident—whether your company is in California or not—you must comply with this legislation. If you're a subcontractor to a company that maintains information about any California resident, you must also comply. This unique approach has made this piece of California law into what has become, in reality, a law that affects most companies in the country. It states that you must give notice whenever an attack has occurred against your network that resulted in personal information being exposed.

"I CAN'T DO THAT"

There are certain things customers don't want to hear someone on the other end of the phone saying:

- **"I can't handle that in this department."** Customers want a seamless experience. They don't care about departmental divisions and office fiefdoms. They just want their problem solved, and they want the first person they talk with to be the one to do it. You must communicate with your employees that you expect them to be able to do this—but then you must also give them the tools and the information they need to make it happen.

- **"I don't know; you'll have to talk to so-and-so."** Employees who give this unpleasant handoff come across as a fool. Not only do they not know how to solve the customer's problem, they are putting the burden on solving it back onto the customer. First of all, the employees should know. Management should have empowered their employees with the information they need or an easy way to access it. If the employee doesn't know the answer, the correct response would be, "I don't know, let me find out the answer for you and get right back to you."

- **"The computer won't let me."** This is the ultimate cop-out, and is sure to make a customer angry. Never, never, never blame the computer. If it's true that the computer won't let you, then you need a new IT staff that can make your computers friendlier. Never arrange your business's processes in such a rigid manner that your employees cannot handle any type of exception

- **"Give me all that information again."** All too often, when customers talk to multiple people in a company, they must provide each contact with their entire story over and over again. When an employee hands off a customer to another employee, the first employee needs to explain to the second employee the nature of the problem and provide him or her with all of the relevant information. There's nothing more frustrating than being transferred to another party, and then having to explain the entire problem again from the beginning.

If you have an integrated system, and empower all of your employees with inter-departmental information, your customers will never have to hear those things.

HIRING CUSTOMER SERVICE PEOPLE

The customer support desk is a vital part of the enterprise and often serves as the first point of contact with customers. The people you employ there must have a service mentality, and more often, companies are requiring specific training and certification for their help desk people. In the tech arena, help desk people are also often required to have a degree in computer science, or at least significant technical knowledge. As industry in every sector becomes more sophisticated, it will continue to become more important to have highly educated, trained, and certified people to handle customer service.

Customer service staff are not the low end of your corporate totem pole. It's an area from which you can groom people for middle- and higher-management, and it's an area that may ultimately make or break you. Customer service is very often the only thing that sets you apart from the competition, and the people who staff your customer service department are an important part of your success. Don't make the mistake of thinking of customer service as a cost center. At the end of the day, this is what's going to keep the paying customers coming back to you. As such, you need to pay your customer service staff appropriately so that you can keep the best ones. It's a competitive field, and the best companies are always looking for good customer service people — often even attempting to lure them away from you with promises of higher pay and greater benefits. Customer service people are professionals, and the only way you will have a professional staff is to pay them like professionals.

CERTIFICATIONS

Certifications have become an excellent and very common way of determining whether a job candidate has a specific skill. There are many technical certifications available that have gained much popularity, such as the MCSE, which lets an employer know that a candidate has met a specific level of competency and is capable of doing the job at hand. But beyond technical certifications, there are also certifications in other areas that can be just as helpful.

While certification doesn't replace the overall experience of a college degree, it does prepare an individual for a very specific slice of work activity. Three types of certifications you may wish to look for in a customer service candidate are:

1. **General customer service/help desk certification.** This type of certification shows that the candidates have undergone a program that has prepared them for the basics of the help desk, including techniques in handling difficult customers, problem-solving techniques, and

some basic phone and computer skills.

2. **Certification for CRM platforms.** Customer relationship management (CRM) platforms often are complex and sophisticated and tie a broad range of services, databases, and technology into a single, unified interface. It brings unity to all customer-facing applications and efficiency to the customer service area. It's also often very complicated to run, and a certification to show proficiency on a given CRM platform may be desirable.

3. **Technology-related certification.** This is necessary only if your help desk people will be offering support for a specific type of technology. For example, if you are a network integrator that installs and supports computer networks, it may be appropriate for you to have customer support people who are certified network specialists.

A WORD ABOUT THE HELP DESK CAREER

The help desk has gone through many changes over the years, and as a career opportunity, it has been seen through different perspectives as well. At one time, the help desk was seen as an entry-level position, and sometimes even as a dead-end job. This is no longer true.

In fact, the help desk today requires a skilled and educated individual, often with specialized certifications and technical knowledge. People in tech support today often move into different positions within the organization. Unlike straight clerical work, the tech support person can and often does move into management and high-end technical positions. The customer support desk has gained a lot of respect over the past few years, and the customer support staffer now makes more money than before, enjoys more status, and has more opportunities for advancement.

Many companies' hiring strategies involve putting recent college graduates into tech support or customer support positions and grooming them for higher-level positions.

BACKGROUND

Besides a certification, a help desk person ideally will have a bachelor's degree, or at least some higher education. Many technical and vocational schools have very good one- or two-year programs for customer service specialties; depending on your needs, this may be adequate.

If your help desk employee is going to be handling technical calls, a technical education is in order. There's nothing more frustrating to customers than trying to talk to a customer support person who knows nothing about the technology they're having a problem with. It's true that your CRM platform will likely provide your customer service people with a tool that lets them walk through several tiers of situations and questions in order to find the solution to a problem, but those platforms should be supplemented with some basic knowledge of the thing you are supporting. It's one thing for help desk people to look on a computer screen that's telling them to ask the customer, "Is your NIC plugged in," but the help desk staff should also understand just what precisely a NIC is used for.

Your support people need a combination of three skills: 1) people skills, 2) customer service skills, and 3) specific technical skills related to your product line.

A BACKGROUND CHECK

Almost all companies do at least a rudimentary background check on a candidate, even if it's only calling the former employer for a reference. Your job candidate may seem to be perfect. He was convincing during the interview, spent several years at blue-chip companies with good written references, and graduated summa cum laude from your own alma mater. His résumé lists membership in several volunteer and charitable organizations, and you're sure you saw him helping an old woman cross the street as you looked out your window after the interview.

But not all is as it seems. Candidates can pad their résumés, and sometimes they are completely fabricated. Vital information may have been withheld, and they may have left their last position under a cloud of suspicion. You want to know something about your candidate's background, and fortunately, you can.

There are a variety of different checks you can have done. Once you've narrowed down your candidate pool to a short list, spend the money to have a service perform these checks. You can have criminal, employment, educational, and even credit checks done on candidates. These screening devices have become more common and more necessary.

A criminal background check is often useful and frequently done by many companies. This isn't to say that one should never give those who have paid their debt to society a second chance, and in many cases, former convicts can make excellent employees. It's a judgment call, but you'll want to know something of the nature of the crime. If they committed a violent act with a handgun, then you probably don't want them on your team. If they spent a week in jail because they had too many traffic tickets or for some other minor infraction, you may want to overlook the criminal record and give them a chance if they seem otherwise qualified.

Credit checks on job candidates have also become common, but it's not necessary for all situations. If the candidate will be handling money in some capacity, it may be worth considering. Some HR specialists claim that candidates with bad credit make bad employees in general, and candidates with the best credit will be more responsible overall. Such claims are misleading at best. Credit problems, especially today, befall even the best of us.

When conducting any type of background check that will access public records, you must adhere to the Fair Credit Reporting Act (FCRA). This applies even if you are not doing a credit check. The Federal Trade Commission says that any public record is considered credit information, and you must therefore obtain written permission from the candidate to perform background checks, and you must give them notification that you intend to use the information in your decision-making process.

Even without hiring the services of a background-checking agency (which is surprisingly inexpensive), you have an easy, quick-and-dirty method that you can use right away, and it's called Google. A quick search on the Internet of candidates' names can often turn up some surprising results. They may, for example, have entries in various blogs throughout the Internet that might give you some insight into their true personalities. They may have published papers that are referred to, and you can often find out much more than you have been told in person through this simple method.

And lastly, a word about "guilt by association." In this age of corporate scandal, this has become an ever-present problem. High-profile and very large corporations have fallen due to corporate mismanagement and outright theft at the highest levels. When that happens, the former employees of the guilty company often have a hard time finding employment in the same field due to guilt by association. Resist the temptation to tar former employees with the same brush as you would their former employers. If the CEO of their former place of employment is currently sitting in prison, does that necessarily mean the job candidates sitting in front of you are similarly guilty of wrongdoing? No, and whether you even consider it an issue will depend on what their position was. Too often, everybody in the fallen company suffers, from the top executives down to the people who take out the trash at night. Yet in many of these cases, whatever wrongdoing transpired took place only in a very isolated area of the company, and most of the other staff were completely unaware of what went on.

You will, of course, want to pay attention when candidates walk into your office having worked for a company that has had such a scandal and determine what their position was and how close they were to the actual wrongdoing. But if your job candidates were not indicted for any of the crimes committed or alleged, it would be unethical to assume that they were involved.

TRAINING

Most customer service organizations will have some sort of information database to which the service person can refer for quick answers to common questions and problems. Nonetheless, there's a lot more to customer service than looking up answers. If that were all there was to it, customer service desks could be staffed with just about anyone capable of reading, but it's just not so. Your customer service people will be taking a lot of simple calls with easy answers, but they will also get some more difficult calls—and must be prepared to handle them when they come up. Your service people must be knowledgeable themselves about your industry and your product line and what your customers are likely to want to do with your products.

When hiring a customer service person, perhaps the most important thing is to find someone that is predisposed to giving good customer service—someone with the right personality to interact with your buying public and to represent your company. The specific skills a customer service person will need, such as running your CRM platform, managing your customer databases, and understanding your phone system, can all be taught later.

It matters a lot less whether the candidate knows all the finer points of how to run an Excel spreadsheet or create a Word document, so don't get caught up in making the all-too-common "laundry list" mistake. This is what happens when a hiring manager expects to hire someone to walk in the door and go to work, without any training, orientation, or preparation at all. The manager expects the customer service person to be familiar with every piece of software the department uses, and therefore makes a checklist that focuses more on the clerical end of the job and not enough on the people end of the job. The result is that the manager hires a lot of very competent clerks, but they tend to lack in the very skills they should have been hired for. In fact, customer service is not a clerical job. Your customer service people represent you and your company, and in many cases, may be the first and only interaction customers have with your company. How they represent your company to the public is a lot more important than whether they are familiar with a particular word processing software program.

ARE CUSTOMER SERVICE PEOPLE MADE OR BORN?

Great artists, it is said, are born, not made. While training can refine these talents in the fine arts, the predisposition to being an artist is something one is born with. Is it the same way with customer service? Can you take people off the street and turn them into good customer service agents? In a word, no.

Customer service training is, of course, an essential part of your operation and is useful for imparting company policy and procedures to your staff. It is useful for training them how to use specific technology tools that you use to deliver customer service, and it is useful in giving your people specific techniques to deliver customer service.

However, there are far too many customer service guidebooks that dole out advice such as "smile to your customer," "have a good attitude," and "make yourself the best you can be." If you must be told these things, then you probably should not be in customer service in the first place.

Because of the difficulty involved in spotting raw talent, hiring customer service people is one of the most difficult tasks a manager can face. Hiring an accountant, for example, is easy, and skills can be easily tested. There are right and wrong answers, and the candidate either knows them or not. Being in customer service is much more subjective, and the customer service agent will face a lot of gray areas over the course of his or her job tenure. And while policy manuals and job descriptions may be useful in giving customer service people a guideline as to what they need to do and how they need to do it, they must have far more discretion than other staff in order to do their jobs correctly.

During the hiring process, there are some things you can look for to improve your chances of hiring a winner. First and foremost, you will want to seek out candidates who are able to think for themselves and make decisions on their own. This is why customer service people make excellent candidates for advancement into management roles (a fact that is often overlooked by HR people). You'll be looking a lot more at the candidate's personality than you would for another position here. While a candidate who is soft-spoken and shy may be an excellent accountant, she would probably not be good in customer service. Look for someone who is well-spoken, takes charge of the conversation, and is aggressive without being annoying. At the same time, the candidate must be able to listen to others and hear what they are saying. Someone who constantly interrupts and won't let the other party speak is going to be over the top and will be a poor candidate for customer service. It's a balance — the ability to listen and the ability to speak are both important.

Still, it's difficult to judge a candidate's personality over the course of a few short interviews. Many successful companies use personality tests with great success. In many cases, these can be purchased by you from a test vendor and administered to the candidate right in your office on a computer.

If you want quality customer service, and all the benefits to your business that entails, then you must have quality customer service people. In your hiring process, treat customer service as a vitally important part of your business that requires skilled personnel. Avoid the temptation to think of it as a "soft" skill that is less important than other skills, such as engineering or accounting.

THE INTERVIEW PROCESS

When you're interviewing for engineers, the questions you ask will tend to be a lot more specific and closed-ended. Above all else, you want to be able to tell if they know how to do very specific tasks involving sophisticated technology. Questions are to the point and answers are brief.

Interviewing customer service people is another process entirely. The best type of questions are open-ended ones, because this gives you a chance to test the candidates' ability to speak and think on their feet. The candidate who gives you nothing but simple yes and no answers will be a poor customer service person.

Staging some problem-solving scenarios may be exceptionally useful and will provide you with some insight as to how the candidate will handle various situations. Describe a situation or two that a customer service person in your organization is likely to encounter, and ask how the candidate would handle it. Better yet, act it out, with you as the customer.

Ask about specifics of their previous positions in customer service, or if they have not been in customer service before, ask about situations they have been in where they have had to deal with a difficult customer. For example, a good question would be, "Tell me about one of the most difficult customer interactions you've ever had." Alternately, let them reverse roles and tell you about an experience they had as a customer somewhere else, where they received poor service.

Most importantly, as hiring manager, you need to spend more time listening and less time talking. Let the candidate take control of the conversation and see where it goes, with you gently guiding it if it gets out of focus. The hiring manager who does all the talking is going to wind up with a bunch of yes-men who will listen to everything he has to say, but will do little to enhance customer service.

CONTINUING EDUCATION

It's just not possible for you to hire people who will be able to walk in your front door and instantly know everything. In addition to a good educational background and training specific to your company, your help desk people will likely need some continuing education. Especially in high-tech companies, where products and technologies are changing constantly, you will need to have periodic in-service training sessions to keep your customer service people up on the latest innovations your product is offering.

Periodic customer service training should be delivered to everyone in your customer center and to selected employees throughout other departments as well. Including other departments in the customer service training will help to promote the teamwork and interdepartmental cooperation that is essential in delivering a good customer service experience. While your customer service department will by necessity be the leaders in providing customer service, the customer service experience should not be isolated to that area. Every department should have a service culture.

You can hold service trainings in-house or, if you prefer, there are many sites where you can send employees to take relevant seminars. In some cases, sending an employee to an off-site seminar can even serve as a reward. But, in addition to in-house or outside courses, you may also do well to provide your employees with a training library.

- **In-house training.** Not all companies have the resources to create and deliver in-house training courses. Resist the temptation to task employees with not enough work to do and make them deliver a course; the results will be disastrous. If you don't have professional trainers on staff, you can easily hire an outside consultant or professional trainer to come into your office and hold the training sessions.

- **Off-site training.** These are plentiful and often inexpensive. It's an excellent option for a smaller organization that lacks a training staff, and employees often enjoy the ability to take time off work to attend an off-site seminar. The downside, of course, is that your staff will be gone for longer periods of time. The solution is to stagger attendance so that each department continues to be covered while individuals attend the sessions.

- **Training library.** Training CDs, videos, books, and interactive tutorials have become very popular, and many of the computer-based training programs have become quite sophisticated. Earlier computer-based training programs consisted of little more than on-screen text, but more modern ones are interactive, contain video sections, and incorporate testing.

While group seminars (on-site or off-site) are, to a degree, social events, use of a training library is solitary and requires more of an incentive to get employees to take advantage of it. Computer-based training can be just as effective as a public seminar, or even more so, because the employee is able to concentrate more fully on the training at hand and work at his or her own pace. Nonetheless, it's often necessary to provide some incentive to get the employees to complete these courses. As we mentioned, attending off-site seminars is often seen as a reward in itself, but completing a computer-based training program may require additional incentives, such as a bonus, a paid day off, or opportunity for advancement.

EVERY EMPLOYEE IS A "CUSTOMER SERVICE" EMPLOYEE

Your goal is to create a company with a service culture. While the focus of this book is on customer service, and this chapter is about hiring customer service employees, in fact, all employees in your organization—whether they deal directly with customers or not—must have a service perspective. Throughout this chapter, we've given some guidelines about how to hire the best customer service employees. Take some of these guidelines to heart when hiring for any position. And while it's probably not necessary for your accounting department to have the same skill set as your customer service department, every single employee in every single department in the organization should nonetheless have the same attitude you are looking for in your customer service staff.

A CHECKLIST

Before you start interviewing, create a checklist to remind yourself of what you are looking for in a customer service employee. Here are a few items you will want to include on your checklist:

- **Education.** The best customer service people will have at least some higher education.

- **Specific skills.** You will need people who understand your product and the technology behind it.

- **CRM skills.** You need people who have a basic understanding of how your CRM system works.

- **Attitude.** It's subjective and hard to pinpoint, but you want someone with a positive attitude who will be ready, willing, and eager to help your customers.

- **Personality.** The right type of personality is essential, not only to serve your customers, but also to function within your organization as a team player.

- **People skills.** Loners may have a place in the corporate structure too, but it's not in customer service. Good customer service people are social beings by nature.

- **Clear background.** Do all the appropriate background checks and ask questions about the candidate's background.

CHAPTER

SWITCHING GEARS

Help desk and customer support people have to wear a lot of hats. Their job description doesn't stop at answering questions and taking orders. Customer service people must, for example, be able to field calls and determine what the customer needs—and either address the situation themselves or escalate the call to another area of the company. The customer-facing agent often has to deal with dozens of different scenarios every day, and keeping up isn't always easy.

Customer service managers and supervisors often make the mistake of focusing on developing their employees' people skills to the exclusion of being able to multi-task and understand what's going on in the rest of the company. Make no mistake, people skills are a number-one priority in customer service. If your staff does not work well with people, if they are surly and grumpy before they've had their morning coffee, and if they take out their frustrations on a difficult customer, then your business will definitely suffer. But it doesn't end there. The customer service person must also act as liaison between the customer and the company, and must therefore possess a thorough understanding of all relevant business processes and workflows. Following are some of the many hats the customer service employee must wear.

THE AMBASSADOR'S HAT: PEOPLE SKILLS

Your sales staff may have closed the deal on the account, but the customer service rep is your company's ongoing goodwill ambassador. No matter how good the salesperson, if a customer gets poor service after the sale is closed, you will lose that customer. In that respect, customer service people should have a bit of the same background and training as the sales staff. Salespeople, at least the good ones, are well known for being able to think on their feet, "schmooze" people when they need to be schmoozed, and carry on a good conversation about any subject. Even if they hate baseball, they still must utter "How about them Cubs?" every now and again. They have a firm but not too tight handshake, and they are a little bit gregarious. They always have a few good jokes memorized for when the occasion warrants it. They know how to "read" a person.

And so it is with a good customer service person. Your customers may have chosen your company because the salesperson impressed them and made them feel welcome. That same theme must continue on through the customer service area.

THE TECHNO HAT

Today's customer service department is filled with modern technology, perhaps more than most other departments.

Customer service staff must be able to manage a sometimes complex CRM system, databases, office productivity software, and various communications software such as instant messaging, e-mail, and real-time chat programs.

And what's more, they must also have a good grasp of the entire technological infrastructure outside of the customer service department, including where they may find all different sorts of information. Customer service is often a funnel point for information, where data must be pulled together from multiple information silos located throughout the enterprise. Hopefully, there will be some integration with the CRM system so the customer service rep doesn't have to juggle multiple applications and logins, or, heaven forbid, walk to the other side of the office to manually retrieve data.

THE THINKING CAP

Automation and CRM systems notwithstanding, customer service is a thinking person's job. In previous chapters, we've forbidden customer service people from saying "I can't do that." An inadequate customer service department might be staffed with individuals armed with all the latest technology, and they may even be technologically adept enough to use it all, but customer service takes people who think "outside of the box." The best technology will take multiple customer scenarios into account, but no piece of software exists that will outthink every customer interaction. Sooner or later, a customer will call in with a request that can't be readily fulfilled with existing customer service business processes. A poor rep would assess the situation and, not being able to find an appropriate box to check, say, "I can't do that." A good one would look beyond the dialog boxes on the computer screen and figure out a way to make it happen.

THE WIZARD'S HAT

When a customer calls in and talks to a customer service rep, that is often the customer's first point of contact. Sometimes it is the only point of contact. The customer has a request, it may be an unusual request for something non-standard, or it may be something that will require cooperation from several different individuals and business processes before it can be provided to the customer. It might be hard to fulfill that request. Customers, of course, do not particularly care how difficult it is or how many different people need to be involved with it, they just want to have their request fulfilled. If there is a problem; they just want it solved. It's the customer service person's job to make it happen, make all the back-end processes and hoops that must be jumped through transparent to the customer, and make it seem as if the customer service person has a magic wand and can wave it and grant the request with little effort, regardless of what it takes to actually fulfill the request.

A SPELUNKER'S HELMET

A customer service rep is the "point man" on the team. When the customer calls asking for something that's not readily obvious, it's the customer service rep's job to go exploring through the darkest recesses of the corporate databases to find it. "What was the amount of my bill for this month ten years ago?" may be able to be discovered with a few mouse clicks, but then again, information that old may have already been archived and taken off the front-line database. The customer service agent must know where to find it, or at least be knowledgeable enough to know where to start looking.

AN ARCHITECT'S HAT

Everybody knows someone who is "the guy who knows where to get stuff." When you need tickets to a sold-out game, an out-of-print book, a rare bottle of wine, or a part for your '62 Studebaker, and you can't find it through regular channels, isn't there always someone who comes to mind? Someone who just seems to have all the answers, who seems knowledgeable on every subject? "I bet Bob would know where to go for that," you say. And sure enough, Bob knows.

A good customer service hiring manager, when "the guy who knows where to get stuff" walks in the door, will hire him immediately. He will quickly familiarize himself with every business process, every department in the company, and every unknown nook and cranny where data exists. The customer service agent, more than almost any other employee, must have a very firm knowledge of the entire operation. He must understand the workflow so that he can pinpoint where a customer's order may be at any given time. He must know people in every department and maybe even develop relationships with your various partners and suppliers so that when cooperation from another department is required to service a customer, he will get it.

A customer service manager must cultivate this ethos by

providing knowledge and training to the customer service staff. Beyond teaching them how to use the software, and imbuing them with obvious slogans such as "always be polite" and "service with a smile," the staff must also be taught about the entire operation, both inside and outside of the customer service department.

FIREFIGHTER'S HAT

It often falls on the customer service agent to "put out fires." When an emergency, or perceived emergency, occurs, customers will contact customer service. "You sent me the wrong part, and I have an order that needs to be filled by tomorrow!" they shout into the phone. Time to slide down the pole and spring into action.

The customer service agent's job isn't just to answer phones and talk to people. Like the firefighter, the customer service agent solves problems quickly. Fulfillment and shipping may be completed in another department, for example—and that would make these tasks ostensibly "not my job" when it comes to a customer service agent. But, in fact, everything is the customer service agent's job. If a customer absolutely needs to have an order by the next day due to an emergency, but the normal process would take two days, it's up to customer service to go to the fulfillment area and make sure that particular order gets moved to the top of the stack, the parts picked from the warehouse, and moved over to shipping right away.

DECISION-MAKER'S HAT

For customer service agents to be able to do all of these things, they have to be given the authority by management to do them. And everybody else must know it. If the parts picker thinks the customer service agent is merely being a nuisance and has no authority, said picker will smile and nod, send the agent on his or her way, and then immediately proceed to ignore the request. The manager must grant authority to the customer service department to:

- Go beyond their normal work processes when necessary to serve a customer.

- Request cooperation from other areas in the enterprise and expect to receive it.

- Go outside of standard procedures when necessary to service a customer.

- Be able to make exceptions within reason when needed to satisfy a customer.

A MIND READER'S TURBAN

Yes, you do need to be somewhat of a mind reader to be a customer service rep. When customers call in, they have an agenda, but they don't always know precisely how to communicate what they want. They may have a picture in their mind of the product they want to order, but they don't know the model number, don't know what it's called, they're not sure whether it's even available separately, and may not even know what it looks like. "You know, it's that *thing*," they say. "The thing that fits into that little piece into the big other *thing* you sell." And they expect you to know what they're talking about.

KEY DRIVERS OF CUSTOMER SERVICE

What drives the customer service process in your organization? In many cases, customer service and the correlating CRM processes are driven by sales and marketing. In a worst-case scenario, the CRM implementation itself is driven by the IT department, which makes for a lot of wonderful and mostly useful whiz-bang technology, but does very little in terms of actually implementing good service.

Some customer service initiatives ultimately fail because of too narrow of a focus. Too often, customer-facing business processes are departmentalized, with data contained in isolated silos of information and individual tasks not integrated with the rest of the operation. Not only does this eliminate opportunities for cross-sell and up-sell, it also disservices the customer who may have requests that require interdepartmental cooperation to take place.

CUSTOMER LIFECYCLE CARE

Going a step beyond CRM is the concept of Customer Lifecycle Care (CLC). CLC bridges the gap that exists between departments and processes, extending CRM into being an interdepartmental initiative that bridges the gap between sales, marketing, customer service, and other departments.

According to CRM vendor RightNow Technologies, Customer Lifecycle Care involves five basic tenets:

1. Give every customer-facing employee a 360-degree view of the customer.

2. Use customer data to optimize business processes and make better decisions on both a tactical and strategic level.

3. Maintain accuracy of customer data to maximize value.

4. Increase revenue generated during post-sales interactions when appropriate with customers throughout the lifetime of the relationship.

5. Leverage customer data to improve customer satisfaction, retention, loyalty, and longevity.

Reprinted with permission of RightNow Technologies, Inc.

CLC is a logical expansion of customer care, since customer care, in reality, goes far beyond the customer service department. While the customer service rep may function as the "point man" or the first point of contact, customer relationships must encompass an interdepartmental focus to be successful.

The CLC concept expands the idea of customer service into every department, making sure that every customer-facing process, regardless of department, is committed to the customer relationship. This concept ensures that information is available at every customer-facing touch point, throughout the entire lifecycle of the customer relationship.

Achieving the 360-degree view of the customer requires some strategy and technology. Business analytics can track the customer interaction lifecycle to make sure that at every customer touch point, customer information is used to the best advantage and new customer information is captured and brought into the system. Further, this information should be available to any authorized employee who needs it to serve the customer, regardless of that employee's job description, department, or link on the customer chain.

EMPLOYEE ENGAGEMENT AND THE CUSTOMER SERVICE CENTER

Employee engagement isn't what happens when you ask your secretary to marry you. It's a business concept that has actually been around for quite a long time but was formalized by business thinker Peter Drucker. It simply means that your employees should not be isolated in their own work areas, but should see themselves as a part of a greater whole. Toward that end, employees should have an understanding of corporate operations outside of their own department. Furthermore, the concept of employee engagement requires a decentralized management focus and a strategy of worker empowerment.

When that customer calls in to your call center, your customer service rep is more than just an employee. To that customer, your customer service reps are the company. They're expected to have all the answers. They are expected to know everything about every aspect of the company, whether it directly relates to customer service or not. Customers may ask things like, "Where do you import those parts from?" "What kind of manufacturing process is used?" or "How come that part costs so much?" The customer service rep should be educated as to the company's operations to the point that those questions can be readily answered out of knowledge and experience. The customer service rep should be able to understand more than just the basic order taking functions. While it's necessary to know whether a particular part comes in blue or whether it works with some other part, knowledge doesn't stop there. Your customer will expect the person on the other end of the phone to be an expert on everything related to your company and its products.

The concept of employee engagement is useful throughout the entire enterprise, but nowhere is the need for it more apparent than in customer service. A customer service person who knows the manual and can look up answers on a database is merely a functionary. Their job could be replaced easily by a computer program. On the other hand, a customer service person who knows your entire operation inside and out, understands the operation, and has a sense of what the company's mission is about, and is empowered to do whatever it takes to get the job done, is truly a solid member of your team, a valuable asset to your company.

How many times have you been in a company where nobody knows what anybody else outside of their area is doing? Many times, no doubt. It's common. The "cubicle syndrome" is one of isolation and a sense of propriety, where employees cultivate a sense of "my area" and "your area." This leads to employees being jealous of their data and processes and a reluctance to seek out assistance and cooperation from other departments.

Rather than "mine" and "yours," a company that has a staff of truly engaged employees will have a sense of "ours." Only when that mindset has been cultivated will you have a truly effective customer service center.

Those customer service reps who are not engaged, and simply rely on functions, processes, and manuals, are the reps who all customers dread talking to. They go by the book. If it's not in the book, then it can't be done. Unfortunately for them, customers will always find a way to make a request that isn't in the book. When that happens, your unengaged customer service rep will diligently check the manual, see that a procedure to handle the customer's request is not there, and promptly report to your customer, "Sorry, I can't do that." Nobody wants to hear that!

Empower your customer service staff to go outside of that manual and policy book. Let them wear many hats. If the solution isn't readily obvious in the standard routine, empower your employee to go outside of the box, work with other departments if necessary, ask others for cooperation and assistance, and find a solution to the customer's problem.

HOW ENGAGED IS YOUR CUSTOMER SERVICE STAFF?

Do you have an engaged customer service staff? Maybe you think you do, but it's the bottom line results and the level of customer satisfaction your company enjoys that really tells the truth about the matter. One tool for gaining an understanding of the extent of engagement is the employee survey.

A brief survey, which is conducted separate from any periodic employee performance reviews, will give you a lot of insight into engagement. Before embarking on such a survey, there are a few caveats to understand. The survey should be informal, and preferably anonymous. Employees should feel free to be honest in their responses, without fear of retaliation or disapproval. Such a survey is meant to provide a general sense of engagement overall, not as a tool for individual reviews.

The results of the survey may tell you, for example, that training in a certain area is lacking. Perhaps your customer service people don't understand how a certain product line works. Equipped with this information, you can then remedy the situation with things like in-house seminars.

Ask some basic questions on the survey, and request that answers be in writing. You can also conduct the survey online. Some questions that would be worthwhile to ask include:

- Do you understand all aspects of your job?

- Do you feel that your job is important to the success of this company?

- Do you understand how to use all of the tools you have at hand for completing your job (software, machine equipment, etc.)?

- Are there other tools you feel should be provided that would enable you to do a better job?

- Are you familiar with all of this company's products and services?

- Do you have a firm grasp of the interdepartmental workflow of all products or tasks that come through your department?

The results can be surprising. You may think you have a skilled staff and they handle everything that comes across their desks very well, but they may not have a clue as to where those tasks came from before they got to them, or what happens to them after it leaves their desks. An empowered, engaged employee understands the entire cycle of every business process with which they are involved.

EMPOWERING YOUR CUSTOMER SERVICE STAFF

If your customer service area is suffering, it may be because your customer service staff does not feel like they have enough authority to go outside the box and fix problems. It could be that they're simply afraid to do something that's not in the manual.

Customer service people should be empowered with the ability to do whatever is needed, and that direction and empowerment should come directly from management. Don't expect them to just understand that they need to solve problems—make it part of the job description, and then overtly grant them the authority to do it. And then make sure everybody else in the company knows that they have the authority to do it.

Not every manager understands how to empower an employee. While some employees will naturally take control of a situation, others need direction and approval. That's why it's important for the manager to take overt action to make sure everybody understands the extent of the customer service agent's authority.

One way to empower employees is through the periodic employee performance review. This regular meeting is, or at least should be, more than just a perfunctory meeting where the employee gets a pat on the back and the standard raise. Of course, it's an opportunity to address issues and problems that have come up since the last review, go over performance and career goals, and praise the employee for outstanding work. All those things are good and necessary, but the performance review can also be an empowerment session. It's probably the best opportunity to discuss the business processes the employee is involved with, and find out how well they are working. Besides the performance of the employee, the performance review should also evaluate the performance of the business processes themselves. This is the time to ask your employees for feedback on ways to improve your processes.

Your employees, whether in customer service directly or not, may too often feel like they are helpless to do anything about a system that is broken or inefficient. During the review process, ask them to provide feedback into these areas. Ask them to outline, in detail, each business process they are involved with, how it works, what tools are used to complete the process, and if there are ways those processes could be improved.

QUALITY GROUPS

Good customer service is an ongoing process, and achieving it means paying attention to continuous improvement. As we've seen in this chapter, customer service involves the entire company. The customer service department must be able to talk to, cooperate with, and gain the support of every other department in the enterprise.

Quality groups have become an innovative way for improving business processes, and these, too, can be used to improve customer service. Creating a customer service quality group that includes personnel from every department will help foster this attitude and promote cooperation. In many cases, employees from other departments may resist cooperating with customer service or resent being asked to do something by a customer service employee who is not their supervisor. Getting interdepartmental cooperation is essential in achieving superior customer service, and participation in a customer service quality group is one way to promote this level of cooperation.

The quality group serves two purposes:

1. To continuously improve the quality of customer service.

2. To promote awareness of the need for cooperation between all departments.

The quality group does not have to be a difficult or time-consuming process. It should be mandated by a member of the executive staff. Without executive buy-in, personnel outside of customer service will resent participation and see it as a waste of time and may even refuse to cooperate.

The group should understand its purpose is to improve the process of customer service. Start out with an explanatory session where specific customer service problems are discussed. Staff outside of customer service may not even realize that these problems exist, and they may hold the key to solving it without even knowing it.

After the explanatory session, the brainstorming begins, with input being sought from every participant, regardless of department or position. With the participation of people from multiple departments, you will get multiple points of view and may well come up with some unique and innovative solutions. All possible solutions should be examined during the session, and an implementation plan should then be created to put the solution into action. The quality group must have "teeth." That is, they must be able to come up with a viable and workable solution, and then be able to put that solution into practice with the assistance and support of the highest level of management.

In addition to directly coming up with solutions, the quality group simply serves the purpose of empowerment and knowledge. People from outside the customer service area who participate in the session will become aware of the need for customer service, the particular challenges being faced, and how their own department or work area can help.

CHAPTER 6

CUSTOMER SERVICE AS AN OPPORTUNITY TO CROSS-SELL AND UP-SELL

When a customer is communicating with a customer service agent, for whatever reason, your company has an opportunity for cross-sell and up-sell. If the customer is calling to place an order, the opportunities are obvious, but the opportunities still exist regardless of the reason for the customer contact. Even a complaint could be turned into a sales opportunity. Train your customer service agents—as well as all employees who have contact with the customer—to recognize these opportunities.

THE VALUE OF EXISTING CUSTOMERS

Any sales initiative will naturally focus on bringing in new customers, but don't neglect the ones you already have. This is your best source of business, and marketing to your existing customer database is going to bring you far greater results.

There's no question that the business environment in just about every sector is more competitive today than it was just a few decades ago. Customer loyalty is down and customer churn is up, and with the Internet, it's easier now more than ever for customers to find a better deal. If your competitor is selling the same product as you for a nickel cheaper, chances are your customers will find this out soon enough. Success in business hinges not only on developing new customers, but also on keeping the ones you have, and making the most out of each customer relationship. Don't be satisfied to sell just one product to customers, when they need something else that you have, which they haven't bought yet.

New customer acquisition is, of course, an important part of any business, but it's by far the most expensive part of sales. Getting a new convert takes a lot more effort, and a lot more money than "preaching to the choir," as it were. That's why it's so important to keep existing customers happy, and to keep them informed as to what new products you have. And that's why it's important to "know your customer" so you can recognize these opportunities:

- **Knowing when customers can make use of a complementary product**; that is, a product that goes along with something they've already purchased. For example, someone who just purchased a cell phone from you may also need a decorative cell phone holder, an adapter, a "hands-free" hookup for the car, and any number of other gizmos that people buy with cell phones.

- **Keeping track of customer usage for consumable products.** Suppose, for example, you have customers who regularly purchase printer ink cartridges. Keep track of sales dates and quantities, and you can get a good idea of when they're about ready to need more. Staying on top of their own needs, and being there when they need you, will keep them from thinking about going to the competition. They may just be thinking about going out to buy some more ink cartridges, but when you call, you save them the trouble of thinking about it—and you get the sale instead of the office supply store down the street.

- **Understand your customer's needs.** Don't just limit your intelligence gathering to what your customers buy. Gain an understanding of why they are buying. What are they using the products for? What are their internal processes as they relate to your products or services? What are they trying to accomplish? Once you understand this, you can become more than just an order-taker, you can be a trusted advisor who can be a real help to their business. Suppose, for example, you run a boutique and sell a lot of teenage fashions. A clueless dad walks in and grabs the first sparkly trinket he sees for his 16-year-old daughter's birthday. Instead of just taking his money, you ask a gently probing question. The item is obviously not for himself, so you ask, "Buying a gift?" Then he responds, "Yes, for my daughter's sixteenth birthday." You are very familiar with teenage styles and offer him advice on what every 16- year-old girl wants, and guide him over to the slightly more expensive selection of teen styles. He takes your advice, she loves it, and you get his return business.

COMPLAINTS

Complaining customers can be one of your greatest assets. Their complaints show you where your service is breaking down, where you can improve, and it can also be an opportunity to make additional sales.

Complaints in and of themselves aren't necessarily a bad thing. It's how you handle those complaints that matters. It's inevitable that no matter how great your products are or how much you strive to please your customers, at some point, someone will be unhappy. If you do nothing, or make only a half-hearted attempt at delivering good service to the unhappy customer in order to remedy the problem, two things will happen. First, you will lose a customer, and lose out on future opportunities for cross-selling and up-selling that customer. Second, you may even lose additional customers due to the fact that your unhappy customer will tell all of her friends and relatives about her unhappiness with your service, and you will lose out on those potential customers as well.

Here are a few tips for responding to a complaining customer:

- **Follow up immediately with personal service.** Make sure that all of your staff is empowered to do so, to avoid an unhappy customer having to wait around for a manager to take care of the problem.

- **Besides taking care of the problem itself, offer an additional incentive for the customer to return — such as a special discount.** In most cases, just a token is enough to show the customers that they really are appreciated.

For example, if you run a restaurant, and customers have been disserviced, give them a coupon for a free dinner at a future date.

- **Make complaining easier.** It may sound counterproductive at first, but think about it for a while. Customers with a complaint, and no outlet for that complaint, are almost surely bound to never return. Customers with a complaint that they can vocalize immediately and get results, may come back and give you more business.

- **Customers aren't, in fact, always right**, but should nonetheless be treated with respect and made to feel that they are valued.

DO YOU WANT FRIES WITH THAT?

Those are the six most important words the fast-food industry ever came up with. This simple cross-sell, which takes the form of this basic phrase that is now uttered by every fast-food jockey who ever wore a paper hat, has probably been responsible for millions of dollars in additional sales every year.

Training your staff to recognize cross-selling opportunities isn't difficult, but it's important, and it can bring in a lot of extra revenue. There is, of course, technology that shows cross-selling opportunities on the order screen, and this would, for example, give a rep on the other end of a phone call a cue that when customers order product "A," they are very likely to also be interested in product "B."

But cross-selling goes beyond the technology that can sometimes enable it. The teenager who took your hamburger order doesn't need a computer to remind him to say, "Do you want fries with that?" He doesn't rely on a screen alert to know that he should offer to "supersize" your order. It's just part of the training to recognize the opportunity and make it part of every transaction.

TURNING A SERVICE CALL INTO A SALES CALL

Every time a customer calls your service department, there's an opportunity for a cross-sell or an up-sell. Let's take a theoretical interaction from a computer software company as an example: A customer calls in to ask for help in making her software perform a specific task. The tech support person recognizes that the version the customer is using is not capable of performing that task, but does offer advice on how to execute a work-around that will accomplish the same results. The work-around is a little awkward, but it solves the problem and the customer is satisfied. The interaction doesn't have to end there. "Our new version has that feature built in," the rep adds. "You can access it directly from the 'file' menu. Would you like to upgrade to the new version? I can do that for you right now."

In this case, not only has your tech support person solved a customer's problem, he has also made a sale.

Making this theoretical transaction possible, however, may require some changes in business processes. If, for example, tech support was not empowered with the ability to make the sale, and the tech support person would have to hand the call over to the sales department, the sale may have been lost because the customer didn't have time to wait. Providing tech support in this case with access to the sales database and the order-taking menu further empowers tech support to solve problems through an up-sell offer.

Remember, your customers want everything to be transparent. They don't care whether the guy on the other end of the phone is in tech support, sales, customer service, or if it's the guy who empties the trash cans, they just want to have their problem solved; they want to buy whatever it is they want to buy; and they want it now, and they want one person to handle everything for them. They don't want to have to repeat information they've already provided to someone else, and they don't want to be handed off to another department. To the greatest extent possible, empower everyone in every department to handle customer problems, provide solutions, and make sales when appropriate.

ASKING QUESTIONS

If you're working fast-food and standing behind the counter, the opportunity for cross-sell and up-sell is always pretty obvious; if the customer orders a medium drink, ask if they'd like to "supersize" it for just twenty-five cents more (or whatever incremental price it may be). If they order a burger, you say, "Do you want fries with that?" But it's not always that obvious.

Sometimes it takes a little bit of conversation and a few probing questions to find those opportunities. Your customer service agent must not only be able to understand what customers are saying, but must also be able to understand what they haven't said yet. There's an opportunity there to be uncovered.

A few well-placed questions about the customer's situation may yield a lot more information than the customer initially planned to give. Here's an example: Suppose you work in the call center of a software company, and a caller asks you how to make the software do a certain task. Instead of a simple answer, saying "Here's how to do that" or "That software doesn't do that," engage the caller a little and find out what specifically she is trying to accomplish with the software. It may soon become obvious that another product would work much better, and you will have a sales opportunity on your hands.

Suppose, again, you're a car salesperson. Your customer asks, "How does that car handle in the winter?" You answer, "Does great, this baby has a nice warm heater; it's a good winter car." But, in reality, the customer wasn't concerned about the heater, and keeps on looking. A better response would be more probing. Find out exactly what the customer needs to do in the winter. A good salesperson would, for example, engage the customer in conversation to find out that the customer lives in a remote, mountainous area, and needs exceptionally good performance to get through heavy snow. The salesperson would then be able to direct the customer to a reliable four-wheel drive model that is well-suited to that specific purpose.

DATA FOR CROSS-SELL AND UP-SELL

Besides "reading" your customer and asking probing questions, part of being able to cross-sell and up-sell as part of the customer service experience is collecting data. We'll talk more about this in Chapter 7, but specifically for the purpose of establishing a basis for cross-sell and up-sell, a good database of customer information is essential.

Companies in every industry miss good opportunities for cross-selling and up-selling on a regular basis. In many cases, data about customers, which would help identify which customers are good candidates for cross-sell and up-sell, is located throughout the enterprise in individual data silos. The result is that it's impossible to get a true 360-degree view of the customer's needs and potential for increased revenue. The insurance industry, for example, has many obvious cross-sell and up-sell opportunities. If clients have a $100,000 life insurance policy, it's possible they need $200,000. If they have car insurance, chances are they need homeowners, health, and other types of insurance as well. But this requires compiling some detailed data about all clients, such as their lifestyle, demographic data, and claims records. Bringing together all of this data and creating a common view is a challenge. Fortunately, tech companies are on top of the situation and have tools available for just such a purpose — to compile customer data and allow the sales staff to predict what the customer is likely to want or need next. While insurance brokers in this case are an essential channel for the insurance company, without a complete view of the customer, a lot of opportunities for cross-selling and up-selling are lost.

BE A CUSTOMER ADVOCATE

When you or anyone representing your company is talking to customers, the impression you want to leave with customers is that you're not necessarily just trying to make a sale, but that you are their advocate. You're looking out for them, their best interests, and trying to find the best product that will serve their needs well. It's the concept of being a trusted advisor, a marketing technique that has been used by financial institutions, such as banks and insurance companies, for decades.

The customer advocate model of doing business naturally leads to a lot of cross-sell and up-sell opportunities; customers are looking to you to be more than just a salesperson, they are looking to you to advise them on what's best. This model is one of the biggest drivers of solid, long-lasting customer relationships, and one of the biggest drivers of sales of ancillary products and upgrades.

Here are a few examples of how being a customer advocate can drive cross-sell and up-sell:

- A bank officer, in talking to a customer, notices that the customer has a large amount of money in a passbook savings account. "You could get a higher rate of return on your money if you invested in one of these other financial products," the banker says, and pulls out the brochures for certificates of deposit, mutual fund investments, and a new bond fund they are promoting.

- Car salespeople are masters of perceived customer advocacy. A customer walks into a new car lot and gravitates toward the car with the lowest sticker price, but the salesperson assesses his customer's true needs very quickly. Noticing his customer's pregnant wife looking around, he says, "You know, we have a good line of SUVs available for a good price too, and they have plenty of room for kids. And they're some of the safest vehicles on the road today." The customer sees that the salesperson is concerned for his future family and takes his advice on the SUV.

- An insurance agent is discussing car insurance with her customer. It's common for insurance companies to offer discounts for customers who have multiple policies, a natural incentive for cross-sell. "If we can move your homeowner's insurance over to our company," the agent says, "I can get you a discount for multiple policies, and you can save money over what you're paying now for the same coverage." The purchase is a no-brainer from the customer's perspective, and the customer is grateful to the agent for helping him save money.

CUSTOMER LOYALTY

You won't have any cross-sell or up-sell opportunities without a loyal customer base to begin with. And of course — you saw this coming — loyalty comes from good customer service.

Dog owners are familiar with how loyal family dogs can be. They are always by your side, always excited to see you when you come home at the end of the day, and love you unconditionally. Even if you forget to feed them, they will still lick your hand. They can be unquestionably reliable, come when you call them, and delight in pleasing you.

Customers aren't like that. In fact, customer loyalty has decreased since the Internet age, due to several primary factors:

increased competition between vendors, impersonalization of commerce, and the ease with which people can find other people selling the same thing at a lower price.

In the business-to-business commerce arena, long ago, there was a greater sense of loyalty to vendors, providers, and partners, just because there was greater value placed on longevity. The reason that value was there was because it was time consuming and expensive to switch gears and find a new provider, and so Joe Factoryowner, who had a small job shop where he made widgets, always bought his parts from the same suppliers, which were all local. The suppliers always sent Joe a box of his favorite cigars as a thank you, and everything went along fine. That is, until Joe discovered the Internet, became a member of an electronic exchange board, and started accepting electronic bids from around the country. When a vendor in another state offered a better price, Joe knew it would increase his bottom line, and he would be able to buy his wife that mink coat she's always wanted; that was it for vendor loyalty. In the big picture, these e-business exchanges provide a lot of benefit, but they ramp up the competition to an order of magnitude higher than it has ever been. The electronic marketplace washes out low-value players very quickly.

The same thing held true in business-to-consumer transactions. The obvious example is the demise of the corner grocery. Let's take Marty's Grocery Store as an example, a small-town, corner grocery across from the elementary school. In the '60s, Marty sold a lot of bubble gum to the school kids after school. Moms would send their kids down the street for a loaf of bread and a gallon of milk. Marty himself worked the counter, and everyone in the neighborhood knew him. He had a good relationship with his customers and thought of them as his friends. But, in the '70s, the SuperMegaGreatDeal Grocery Warehouse opened. They had everything imaginable, and they sold bread and milk as loss leaders. Marty couldn't compete, and nice guy that he was, he wound up closing his store and working the deli counter at SuperMegaGreatDeal.

The lesson here, cynical though it may be, is clear: Customer loyalty is not a fuzzy, feel-good kind of thing. It's something you plan for and create. It can be bought. You don't get it because you're a nice guy or because you belong to the same lodge as your customer. You get it because you provide good quality products at competitive prices, superior customer service, and rewards or incentives for customers to keep coming back.

CUSTOMER INCENTIVES: BUYING LOYALTY

It's been done for as long as there has been commerce. In the old days, it may have been something as simple as a calendar with pretty pictures given to the best customers during the holidays. In the donut shop, it's the extra glazed donut the lady at the counter puts into your box of a dozen. Big grocery stores buy loyalty by providing customers with special cards that give them discounts at the checkout. One grocery store that also sells gasoline automatically tallies customers' purchases throughout the month, and if they spend more than a hundred dollars, they get ten cents off per gallon.

E-businesses operating on the Internet are well aware of the need to buy loyalty. Online customers are perhaps the most fickle of all, but you can still retain loyalty — and enjoy the cross-sell and up-sell opportunities that result. Here's an example: If you create a targeted e-mail marketing program, you want customers to at least open your emails and not ignore them as spam. Online companies like Mypoints (**www.mypoints.com**) have sprung up to help online companies create loyalty through earning "bonus points." These are like the old-fashioned trading stamps that brick-and-mortar retailers used to give out with purchases. Customers are able to sign up with the program at no cost, earn points for looking at specific ads and e-mails, and earn additional points for purchasing. When they save enough points, they can cash them in for a reward.

Naturally, everybody likes to get something for nothing, and that's why programs such as these have been so successful. By offering this small reward, you get more customers to look at your ads; you get more customers to buy, and you get more customers to come back to you, because they know you are a member of the network of merchants from whom they can earn additional points.

STICKY WEB SITES

In the world of online commerce, having a loyal customer base requires creating a "sticky" Web site. This simply means creating a Web site that people will continue returning to, time after time.

The first step in creating a sticky Web site is to have quality products at competitive prices, and to offer superior customer service. But it goes beyond that. The "stickiness" of your Web site will translate to more cross-sell and up-sell as a natural result of people coming back more often than they normally would.

One thing to remember is that even though a lot of people buy online, Internet users still see the Internet primarily as a source of information. Let's say, for example, that you have a Web site where you sell outdoor pool supplies. You have excellent prices, of course, and deliver promptly. But once your customer gets his equipment and goes out into his backyard with a shovel, things get a little hairy. "What do I do now?" the customer asks his wife, neighbor, and his wise uncle down the street. Unhappily, nobody knows. So the customer goes back to your Web site — and gets what he wants. Why? Because you have provided quality content on your site along with your products for sale. You have several original articles about building and maintaining a backyard pool, complete with diagrams and photos. Of course, as customers read the material and look at the pictures, they'll soon discover that they want or need something else, and they will buy it from you.

That's the added value. It's the extra donut that keeps them coming back. Provide quality content relevant to what you sell, on your Web site directly, through a customer e-mail newsletter, or both, and your sales will increase substantially. By providing quality, useful content relevant to your products, your customers will no longer just see you as a source for products, they will see you as the expert on those products. You will be the "wise uncle" who knows how to do things.

Often, you must position yourself as an expert through the help of others. You may be very good at selling backyard pond supplies, but you don't know a thing about how to actually put one together, and the one time you tried it, your pond dried up and your goldfish died. That doesn't matter. The world is full of experts, many of whom are professional writers. This is the time to discover the wonders of ghostwriting. If you are a great salesperson but not a professional writer, hire somebody who is. Most of them work on a freelance basis and you can negotiate rates. Once you have a large collection of valuable and relevant articles, you can create your content site, and start positioning yourself and your company as the expert in the field. The practice of ghostwriting — which is when a writer creates the content but you, the business owner, put your own byline on it — is widely accepted and practiced by even the largest of corporations. Most books, papers, articles, and manuals with bylines of prominent CEOs were actually ghostwritten by other people. This practice serves the purpose of getting you quality content and positioning you as the expert. That will keep your customers coming back. That's how to buy loyalty.

Advent Software

Advent Software provides reliable software solutions to investment management organizations. The company helps its more than 4,000 client firms improve operational efficiency, reduce risk, and free up investment managers to focus on what they do best.

Advent Software is a customer-focused organization. According to Anthony Sperling, Advent's Vice President, Professional Services, "Customer service is a shared value of the entire organization. While it is often thought of as a function of our services organization—or those departments that specifically exist to install software, respond to customer calls, and create custom applications—we like to apply the principles of great customer service to the entire organization." In addition, Advent management recognizes that the "customer" is everywhere: "We recognize that organizations that produce the most avid fans of their business and brand treat each interaction with other employees, prospective customers, suppliers, and clients alike, as an opportunity to increase the level of relationship that they have."

As a technology company, Advent Software takes full advantage of technology in delivering superior customer service. These technologies include a sophisticated Cisco IP Call Center for intelligent routing—this system delivers calls to specific service reps, based on client information, to expedite client issues. "We've found this delivers a better level of service than having all calls come into one pool of service reps," said Sperling. For non-critical issues, the Web is used to interact with customers as well, through a Web form that walks customers through a series of steps and directs them to specific reps based on their question. Clients don't need to enter in redundant information because the forms are interfaced with Advent's CRM system so the forms get pre-populated with a client's information. Their customer Web portal is also quite thorough. This portal gives clients a convenient online service center for downloading software, receiving patches and upgrades, and a place to search for product documentation and industry articles. To make it more specific to each customer, their "client concierge" provides each client, based on their profile, with information specific to the products they own. Advent also regularly uses e-mail to alert clients to changes in software or available updates, and a real-time dashboard for hosted services.

Even in areas as arcane as software development, the customer comes first. Advent uses a process called "product validation," where developers work directly with clients and prospective clients to develop prototypes of products that will meet the needs of those businesses. Those firms become beta testers of the products, and provide Advent with feedback through the entire development process.

Customer service is an institutionalized process throughout the entire organization—meaning that every person at every level has customer service in mind. This includes top management. "Executive management considers customer service to be a priority," said Sperling. "From meeting one-on-one with clients, to participating in the product validation process to reviewing the results of surveys, Advent's executive management is involved in almost all aspects of how we work with our clients." Sperling adds, "While many of our competitors rely on specific people to deliver consistent quality service, we've invested in processes that will ensure our high level of service regardless of what happens with any one individual at the company." The company has also achieved the Support Center Practices (SCP) certification, which quantifies the effectiveness of the company's support organization.

Sperling summarizes his company's approach to customer service by saying, "Quality service means meeting or exceeding client expectations at each interaction or opportunity. It means to build a network of fans of your brand. The quality of our service is best measured directly from the consumers of the service, but can also be gauged through industry certifications and service monitoring. By building a community of satisfied clients and fans, we attempt to attain greater client loyalty, employee satisfaction, and maximum revenue."

GATHERING INFORMATION ABOUT YOUR CUSTOMERS

You can improve your customer's experience by gaining a better understanding of their needs. Who is your customer? Today's technology gives you a great opportunity to know more about each person who calls into the service center or drops by your Web site. Even before the age of technology, "know your customer" has always been a key to success.

WHERE DOES THE INFORMATION GO?

Okay, you've gotten the idea of gathering customer information. Most departments in your organization do so to one degree or another, and for the most part, find it useful, but where is all that information held? A lot of times, it's held in individual databases, which are useful for specific purposes, but are not so good for the enterprise as a whole. This is where the concept of the data warehouse comes in.

This is a technical concept that attempts to unify corporate data so that all departments can make better use of it, and, ultimately, gain a marketing advantage and better serve customers by being better informed about their needs. The technical end of setting this up could fill several books, but think of it this way: every department generates their own data. Instead of each department keeping data in a separate database that is not connected to the rest of the enterprise, they keep it in a database that is compatible with everybody else's database, and it is either stored in a central "data warehouse" or in a "virtual data warehouse" that connects each separate database so that it functions as if it were a single store. Through the use of authorization and authentication technology, everybody in the enterprise, regardless of department, can get access to whatever information they require, without having to individually plead their case to each department head.

"IT'S ALL IN MY HEAD"

Customers like familiarity, and the fact is it works to your advantage as well. Customers like it when they see the same clerk, the same waitress, or the same serviceperson every time. If you've hired good people, they will develop relationships with your customers over time. It doesn't mean that you have to be best friends with everyone who walks in the door, but that familiarity will engender trust.

Staff persons, whether directly involved in customer service or not, when having worked for you over a long period of time, will get to know their customer's preferences, likes, and dislikes. They may remember most of their names, what kind of cars they drive, and whether or not they have kids. Take the following scenario, for example: A man walks into an auto parts store to buy some oil. The salesperson greets him, and says, "Hey, how did that new car stereo you got last week work out for you?" "Just great," he says, "but now my kid wants one." "Oh sure," says the clerk. "He's seventeen now, right? How's his old jalopy holding up?" And so on. The customer walks out with his oil, but also has it in his mind now to return later to buy his kid a new car stereo.

A second, more impersonal salesperson who merely sells the customer his oil may be perfectly functional, give "service with a smile," and has done nothing wrong, but without that little interaction, the second salesperson will make fewer sales.

The key to promoting this interaction is longevity. Having a lot of employee churn—a "revolving door" if you will—doesn't give your staff enough time to get to know your customers. You may have all the technology and customer databases in the world, but without a staff that has personal knowledge of, and familiarity with, your customers, it won't do nearly as much good.

LEGISLATION

There is a significant amount of legislation, both existing and proposed, that governs the data about your customers that you can collect and save. Much of it is designed to protect financial information and protect against identity theft.

One piece of proposed legislation, known as the Personal Data Privacy and Security Act of 2005, was designed by Senators Arlen Specter and Patrick Leahy to help protect consumer privacy. Senator Leahy refers to insecure databases as "low-hanging fruit" for thieves looking for identities to steal and fraud to commit. He notes that there has been a significant rise in organized crime rings that look for ways to steal this sort of personal data and sell it in online criminal bazaars. The legislation would require companies to give notice to their customers whenever a breach of security occurs that exposes their personal data. The bill would also address poor security and lack of accountability. The legislation forbids the display and sale of social security numbers without consent, and prohibits companies from requiring people to use their social security numbers as account numbers. It also prohibits the practice of requiring a consumer to provide a Social Security number as a condition of service, except for the case of background checks, consumer reports, or law enforcement.

Other existing legislation, such as the Gramm-Leach-Bliley Act and the Health Insurance and Portability Act, also governs use of private customer records.

Some larger corporations have taken the step of appointing a "Compliance Officer" to make sure that they are in compliance with all legislation and are in a good position to comply with legislation that is pending and likely to be approved. Smaller companies can also take steps by adhering to best practices in security when storing and using customer information, such as is outlined by VISA in the next section.

CREDIT CARD INFORMATION AND OTHER LEGALITIES

In addition to legislation, credit card companies also have

standard practices to which you must adhere regarding maintenance of customer financial information.

When your customers pay with credit cards, it's common sense that you don't really need to keep their account information after you've already processed the transaction. VISA USA's VISA Cardholder Information Security Program (CISP) protects cardholder information and requires companies to maintain a standard of information security and to safeguard customer data.

CISP outlines a data security standard with 12 best practices that are required of all processors. These best practices revolve around good security, restricted access of information, and protection of stored data. The requirements are as follows:

1. Install and maintain a firewall configuration to protect data.

2. Do not use vendor-supplied defaults for system passwords and other security parameters.

3. Protect stored data.

4. Encrypt transmission of cardholder data and sensitive information across public networks.

5. Use and regularly update antivirus software.

6. Develop and maintain secure systems and applications.

7. Restrict access to data by business need-to-know.

8. Assign a unique ID to each person with computer access.

9. Restrict physical access to cardholder data.

10. Track and monitor all access to network resources and cardholder data.

11. Regularly test security systems and processes.

12. Maintain a policy that addresses information security.

The third and fourth requirements in particular are relevant to your stored customer data. Obviously, when a customer makes a transaction, you want to make a record of that transaction. This information is invaluable for tracking sales trends and for offering better customer service. But success is dependent not just on what you keep in that database, but also on what you do not. Millions of cardholder account numbers, names, and other data have been exposed to attackers because companies, very often large companies that should know better and have the resources to implement strong security, neglect to protect this basic information. The FTC has been aggressively levying steep fines against companies whose data security has been inadequate, resulting in exposure of personal customer information.

VISA makes some very specific recommendations in terms of your stored data. First, cardholder information storage should be kept to a minimum. Companies must have a data retention and disposal policy regarding this information, such that account information is retained only as long as it is necessary for business, legal, or regulatory purposes. Furthermore, VISA's CISP requirements call for companies to not store the full contents of any track from the credit card's magnetic strip, not store the card validation code, and not store the PIN verification value.

It is also necessary to mask account numbers whenever they are displayed. Typically, only the last four digits are displayed. Any sensitive cardholder information that must be retained for any period of time should be encrypted through either one-way hashes, truncation, index tokens and PADs, or strong cryptography.

Regarding the fourth requirement, all cardholder and sensitive information must be encrypted when sent across a public network. This is an absolute necessity. Hackers can very easily intercept data while it is being sent; sending cardholder data in the clear is a disaster waiting to happen.

COOKIES

Much has been written and debated about the use of cookies, which are small files that are created and stored locally for the purpose of recalling specific data. Cookies serve many useful purposes. For example, if you are a consumer and you return periodically to a given Web site, the cookie will allow that Web site to remember who you are and what your preferences are. This is what allows opening Web pages to greet a customer by name and remember preferences. It's possible to create a Web page that is tailored to each individual user with the help of cookies. They are also very useful in tracking user behavior, such as how often people visit your site, what pages they visit, and so forth.

For the most part, they are not used to gather specific personal financial data that could be misused; the greatest use of cookies by far is tracking usage trends. By tracking usage trends, it is possible to determine what users like and dislike, and therefore refine one's Web site to better serve customers.

However, the use of cookies can be abused, and a great many users take exception to the use of cookies, and either prohibit their use or regularly delete them.

It's important to differentiate between first-party and third-party cookies. A first-party cookie is placed on the local computer by the Web site the user is visiting. Those are the ones that preserve user "state" and generate the friendly greetings that call the user by name. These are the most useful and least offensive. Third party cookies are often placed by ad companies or analytics firms, and they are used to track a user's behavior over time. These are sometimes used to serve pop-up ads, spam, and other types of electronic junk mail. You can also divide them into enabling or monitoring cookies. An enabling cookie is the useful variety that remembers work preferences for each end user. The monitoring cookies watch behavior. But because of misuse, about 40 percent of all online users simply reject or delete all cookies and disregard the positive aspect of these little files.

WHO ARE YOUR OFFLINE CUSTOMERS?

Despite the complications and privacy concerns over cookies, it's still relatively simple to gain a good understanding of your online customer. Even without the cookies, Web analytics software can allow you to track how your Web site is generally used. You can determine which pages are looked at the most often, where users come from, and what they do while they are on your site. It's like assigning an invisible employee to walk behind all customers who walk into your store and record everything they do on a note pad. Of course, in the brick-and-mortar world, you can't do that, so one must resort to other means to gain an understanding of and to track your customers.

Of course, if yours is largely a credit/account based business, you will have records of customer information, addresses, and buying histories attached to each customer, but what about your cash business? If you have a small shop, for example, much of your business is just walk-in and largely anonymous. If you own a boutique, people — whose names you do not know — will occasionally walk into your store and buy scarves, jewelry, and handbags. Sometimes you will notice the same ones come in more than once, but even so, tracking that kind of traffic is difficult. It's left up to you as the shop owner, or your employees, to notice who comes in on a regular basis and remember what they like and dislike.

But beyond just having a good memory for faces, there is still more you can do. A popular technique is to publish a regular newsletter. This works especially well if you are in a business that requires some information. For example, if you run a hardware store, you could create a newsletter with fix-it tips. If you run a gourmet grocery store, publish a newsletter with exotic recipes. If you have a travel agency, publish a newsletter with exciting travel articles. Have a sign-up on your Web site and in your physical storefront, where people will leave their names, physical addresses, and e-mail addresses.

Of course, grocery stores have come up with the best idea yet with the discount cards that many offer now. You simply sign up for a card and use it every time you shop, and then you get to take advantage of sale prices on certain items. They've become so commonplace that people keep them on their key chains for easy access. Of course, at first glance, it seems like it's simply a way to give people discounts, but in reality, grocery stores have used coupons, discounts, and sales long before these cards became popular. Their main purpose is tracking. With these tools, the grocery store can tell easily how much you usually spend, how often you visit the store, and what brand of toothpaste you use. The marketing opportunities here are endless. And as a customer service tool, it's the best way to know your customer. With the information they are able to gather through use of these discount cards, grocery stores can tell which items are popular and refine their inventory over time to serve customers better with a progressively improved stock. In addition, the computer could be programmed to generate store coupons customized to each buyer. If, for example, you buy three jars of peanut butter every week, the store could program the computer to print out a coupon for jelly and bread at the point-of-sale (that's up-sell again!).

The discount cards generated by grocery stores do require some significant investment, but there are less expensive alternatives for the smaller business. The "buy ten, get one free" punch card is a simpler equivalent. Simply print up cards, at your local print shop or with a high-quality photocopy machine, with ten empty spaces. Your customers sign up to receive a card, and every time they shop, you punch out one of the spaces. When it's full, they get a reward—a free item, a discount, or something of value. Besides the marketing value here, like the grocery store discount card, it's a good customer service tool. Customers are, of course, always happy when receiving a bargain, or receiving something for free. People like to get rewards. It also lets you know your customer better; it gives you an opportunity to tell who shops more frequently than others, and gives you an opportunity to create a customer database by requiring them to provide their name and address to receive the card.

CHAPTER 8

CRUNCHING THE NUMBERS

E very time a customer service call occurs, a log of that experience should be entered. Record the nature of the call, what the results were, and whether the customer left the call satisfied. Other details like length of call, time on hold, and whether the call had to be escalated to another level are also useful. This information is very helpful in spotting trends and understanding what is working and what's not in the customer service center.

What we're talking about is called business intelligence, or business analytics. And, yes, there's software for this too. You must be able to understand your customer-facing departments, customer behavior, and their wants, needs, and demands.

WHAT YOU NEED TO KNOW

A tremendous amount of data is generated from all of your customer-facing applications. This information can be sliced, diced, compiled, and analyzed to help you make more sales and help you serve your customers better.

It's not enough to know that you're probably doing a "pretty good" job because you don't get too many complaints. You need to get specific.

WEB ANALYTICS

The Web is a major sales channel and a major customer service channel. It is where many of our customers turn when seeking information about us or our products. A company's Web site is its virtual ambassador to the world; it is, for many consumers, the first point of contact. It is where your company gets introduced to potential buyers.

What happens on that Web site is of vital importance. It is not enough just to put up a Web site with a lot of good information and customer features.

Web analytics is a method of gathering information from visitors to your Web site. This information is parsed into easy-to-read graphs and reports, which lets you spot trends and better understand the people that visit your site, what they want to do, and how you can better serve them.

There are a number of Web analytics tools available, and some Web hosts even offer a basic hosted Web analytics service that lets you log in to get a basic report of your Web traffic. These tools let you identify things such as:

- What domain visitors came from.

- Which are your most popular pages.

- A ranking of your most common landing page.

- Which pages each visitor looked at.

Most of these tools will also further analyze this information to help you refine your site and spot trends. For example, you can use this information to determine which states most of your visitors live in and which pages are viewed most often. It can also tell you which pages are viewed less often, which is useful information as well because it tells you which pages you need to work on. You can also use this information to spot correlations; for example, it may tell you that most visitors who went to page X also went to page Y.

While Web analytics is often posed as a marketing tool, it is also useful as a customer service tool since, ultimately, it is allowing you to better serve your customers by offering them a Web site that is more likely to be useful to them.

There are several hosted Web analytics services as well as software that you can run yourself. But Google, being the powerhouse that it is, deserves special mention with their recent release of Google Analytics, a groundbreaking free service that you can use to analyze these trends on your Web site. The service is based on the technology Google acquired from a company called Urchin. It is very useable and an excellent way to get started with analytics. It is especially useful for small- to medium-sized Web sites. There are other analytics services with more high-end features, but this is an excellent product for most needs. And, of course, being free makes it an even better deal for smaller businesses that have to watch their IT budgets.

CRM ANALYTICS

This is where you will gain an understanding of customer behavior. What are your customers' demands? Not only should you be able to know what they are, you should be able to know what they are ahead of time. This sort of analytics focuses on three areas: 1) service, 2) sales, and 3) marketing.

- **Service analytics** lets you know if your customers' expectations are being met and whether agents are meeting stated service goals. You should be able to measure things like average response time, first contact resolution rates, service level achievement rates, and agent effectiveness.

- **Sales analytics** improves the accuracy of your sales forecasting by giving you real-time visibility into your sales pipeline. With sales analytics, you can identify opportunities for new revenue, improve the effectiveness of your sales organization, and increase your close rate.

- **Marketing analytics** helps you better understand your marketing campaigns with end-to-end tracking. This is the tool you use to determine which of your customers are most profitable and which are your lowest value customers. You should also be able to get an understanding of your peak inquiry loads and see how effective your answers are on your online self-serve Web site.

CUSTOMER FEEDBACK

You can learn a lot from talking to your customers. You can

learn even more from a formal customer survey or focus group. Getting customer feedback can take the form of a simple survey that can be sent via e-mail or handed to customers physically at your brick-and-mortar location. You can send it to them with their invoices. Restaurants sometimes put survey cards on the table or on the back of a receipt. Just get it to them, one way or the other. Offer an incentive for completing the survey in the form of a coupon or free item. You may be very surprised at the results, and you're very likely to find areas that you can improve your service to customers, offer them more products and services they want, and increase sales. Some questions to ask in your survey may include:

1. What matters most to you about the service you receive?

2. How well do we deliver that service?

3. Is there anything you'd like to see in your customer experience that we're not delivering?

4. Are there any products that you would like for us to carry that we don't have?

5. If there is one thing you could change about how we do business, what would it be?

6. What do you like most about the service you receive from us?

7. What do you like least about the service you receive from us?

Try to come up with open-ended questions, but don't be too

generic. Just asking "How's the service?" will generally elicit a half-hearted answer. The casual "How was your dinner?" that is asked as you walk out of the restaurant is more of a nicety than a real question. It's like asking someone you meet on the street, "Hi, how are you?" The answer will inevitably be "Just fine," regardless of that person's actual state at the time.

Ultimately, good customer service flows from knowing what customers want and what they think about your company and the service they receive. For this reason, you must open a dialogue between your company and your customers. Make it easy for them to contact you, and make it easy for them to respond to your survey.

CHAPTER 9

YOUR NEIGHBORHXOOD CALL CENTER–NOW CONVENIENTLY LOCATED IN INDIA

When is outsourcing customer service a good strategy? This has become very common for companies of all sizes. Small companies, in particular, are embracing the outsourcing model for customer service, a strategy that allows them to have the equivalent of a customer service department when one would not be affordable otherwise.

For some, an initial knee-jerk reaction is to condemn the practice of outsourced customer service. Somehow, it seems like cheating. It's seen as a quick fix, in the same category as downsizing, and as a way to line the pockets of the executive staff. Indeed, a common cry in the employment arena is "I've been outsourced!" Certainly not an attractive scenario if you are the one whose job has just been sent to another country.

In reality, in many cases, outsourcing your customer service is a strategy that will result in better and more accessible customer service, and, ultimately, customers who are happier and better served than they otherwise would be if your customer service was in-house. This is especially true with smaller companies and companies experiencing rapid growth. Implementing an in-house customer service center is not a simple task. It requires hiring and training staff and a significant investment in technology. It requires a big monthly expenditure in telecom, not to mention the extra office space involved. It's better to hire a professional third party to handle the function, and have it done correctly and efficiently, as opposed to doing a half-hearted job of it in-house.

The outsourcing of customer service has gained significant attention over the last few years, as large call centers in India and elsewhere offer excellent services with skilled, English-speaking personnel. Advances in telecommunications make it easy to create a call center where, for example, your customers dial a toll-free number, or even a number with an area code that would make it seem like they are dialing your U.S. headquarters, but in reality, that call is routed to a call center on the other side of the world.

FAILED OUTSOURCING PROJECTS

According to Gartner Group, 80 percent of organizations that attempt to implement an outsourced customer service center, in order to minimize costs, will fail. Whether you are outsourcing offshore or domestically, there are bound to be a few hiccups along the way, and there are a few things to watch out for. Gartner notes that through 2008, 60 percent of organizations that outsource customer-facing processes will have customer defections and other hidden costs that will offset, to at least some degree, the savings realized from outsourcing.

To be sure, there are risks associated with outsourcing the customer service function, and not approaching the outsourcing from a strategic perspective will often result in failure. One of the greatest mistakes is to approach it with a set of goals that are poorly defined. Without the right information to make a good cost/benefit analysis, a company may instead go into outsource contracting with service and cost goals that cannot be easily measured.

An outsourcing model that is not managed correctly can result in increased costs, reduced quality of customer service, and dilution of your company brand.

Two other common tactical errors are 1) entering immediately into a long-term outsourcing contract, and 2) not conducting an initial pilot program to gauge the success of the outsourcing initiative. Instead, approach outsourcing the customer service function in phased steps.

Another common element of failed systems is a company that fails to make a detailed assessment of transitioning the function to the outsourcer, how information and processes will flow back and forth, and how well you are able to manage your outsourced relationships.

AN OUTSOURCING STRATEGY FOR SUCCESS

If implemented correctly, outsourcing customer-facing processes can lead to improved service and cost savings of up to 25 percent or more. The key to saving money with outsourcing, however, is not to expect immediate results.

Outsourcing your customer service function can be an excellent decision if done correctly, for the right reasons, with the right agency, and in a phased approach. The following are some recommendations for a successful outsourcing initiative:

1. **Outsourcers often have high attrition rates.** Before selecting an outsourcer, find out about their staff attrition rates. If they have a constant revolving door of customer service reps, they are a lot less likely to have skilled and experienced people on hand who are familiar with your company and your products, regardless of any training that you provide.

2. **Take a hands-on approach to managing your outsourcing contracts.** Create a contract with distinct performance objectives and metrics that must be met as a condition of the contract. Consider your third-party outsourcer as an extension of your own company. Schedule regular meetings to review performance as well as the needs of both parties. In addition to specific performance objectives, include quality of service objectives as well.

3. **Map out your customer-facing processes, and ensure that you are planning for a seamless flow of information and service.** At some point, there is a handoff of customer information between you and the outsourcer, and then a handoff in the other direction. There may be multiple flows of information going in both directions and physical exchanges of paperwork. Make sure each of these flows is documented and organized in such a way that it seems like a seamless transaction to the customer.

4. **Monitor the performance of the outsourcer with a post-contact customer survey.** When customer service is done in-house, it's always easy to know when an agent is not performing well, but will the third-party outsourcer tell you? Probably not; they would see an underperforming agent as an internal personnel matter for them to take care of in-house on their side.

5. **Realize, above all, that the outsourcing process will take time.** There's a lot more involved than bringing over a cardboard box full of files and a database and expecting the third-party company to take it over. Plan for a transition period, and expect there to be a few glitches along the way. Don't expect an immediate return; see it as a long-term investment.

6. **With outsourcing of any type, although it does take the burden of production off of the company, an attitude of "it's your problem now" should never be taken.** The process, regardless of the degree of outsourcing, is always your own, and should be treated as such.

7. **Know your outsourcer's degree of professionalism.** Do they hire anybody off the street to run the phones? Find out ahead of time whether they employ professional, certified, and trained help desk personnel.

WHAT TO OUTSOURCE

"Let's outsource our customer service" is simply too broad a statement to make sense. Customer service is, in fact, made of several discrete processes and different levels. Let's first separate customer service into two "piles" of processes: 1) processes that can be outsourced, and 2) processes that can be automated. There are, of course, situations where your customers need to hear a human being on the other end of a telephone, and this is a process that can readily be outsourced. It can be successful, given a good relationship with a quality outsourcer.

But, in fact, the vast majority of customer center calls are very routine. Not all calls require technical knowledge, troubleshooting, or extensive problem solving. It may be a simple, "How do I make the software do this?" "What is my account balance?" "Can I make a payment online?" or "Can I exchange this for a red one?" Do you really need a live person to answer these questions? No, not really.

To be sure, there will be some customers who will use the live call center for even the smallest and most routine question, and they should be accommodated. But most customers would prefer to avoid the wait on hold and either look up the answer on your Web site or seek an automated answer. There's no need to funnel all of those routine calls to your third-party customer service outsourcer when there's a less expensive and more efficient alternative in automation.

Web-based customer service, or e-service, leaves the humans to handle the more complex calls, and automates everything else. Don't overlook the Web as a tool for customer service. Many customer queries can be answered online in an automated fashion through tools like online FAQs. Alternately, they can be handled through telephony technology such as interactive voice response (IVR) or touchtone response and recorded answers. If a customer is unable to find the answer they needed through your automated system, then the call can be handed off to the live agent.

WHERE TO OUTSOURCE: OFFSHORE OR DOMESTIC OUTSOURCING

The market for customer service outsourcing continues to grow and is projected to reach over $12 billion by 2007. But, of that, the offshore element is comparatively small, representing just 2 percent of the market in 2005. Gartner projects this to increase to somewhat less than 5 percent by 2007.

Gartner also notes that outsourced contact centers have higher staff turnovers, and many of the Indian-owned business process outsourcing startups that offer customer service outsourcing will likely be acquired, merged, or marginalized.

That said, the Indian IT community is without a doubt one of the most highly skilled in the world, and if you are going offshore, this is definitely the place to start looking. The English language skills of the call center reps there are typically excellent, sometimes with staff members who speak English without even a trace of an accent. Higher education in India is similarly of a very high quality, and a staff person with a degree in IT from a top Indian university will be every bit as knowledgeable as a graduate from MIT. It is a young market still, though, and like young market segments in the United States, will undergo a shakeout of sorts. This is inevitable, in India or anywhere else in the world. The result will ultimately be a smaller number of larger, more skilled, and highly professional outsourcing centers capable of meeting your customer service needs at a very competitive price.

WHY OUTSOURCE

Before you've decided what to outsource and where to outsource it, the key thing to consider is, Why do it? The answer that first comes to mind is to save money. Although this can be a very desirable benefit of outsourcing the customer center, it's not the only reason, or even the main reason. At the end of the day, you may even come out even financially, but there are other reasons to outsource.

Startups, especially high-tech ones, must go from 0 to 60 in under a minute, so to speak. In order to survive, one must hit the ground running, and be able to operate as a company without a long ramping period. In many cases, the only way to do this is through outsourcing non-core functions. Smaller companies and startups often lack the resources to implement a full-scale customer service center, and outsourcing provides an excellent opportunity for them.

And, of course, smaller companies are less able to afford high-end CRM systems. Larger companies typically spend millions of dollars on software and integration costs alone when implementing CRM, and the CRM market as a whole has only until recently been focusing exclusively on the high-end, leaving small businesses very little to work with outside of common desktop productivity applications. For a smaller company, implementing a full-fledged, all-out CRM system may break the entire IT budget.

Saving money is, of course, a powerful incentive. There is an increasing globalization and greater competitive pressures on business today than there has ever been, and this has been a major driver in the trend toward outsourcing. In recent years, the concept of the "virtual" company has taken hold, and several successful companies operate with minimal office space or none at all, relying on the Internet as a unifying factor. Outsourcing is a natural for the virtual company.

Like it or not, globalization is not just a passing phase, it's a part of life, and it will have an increasing impact on your business. It creates competitive pressures that didn't exist before. Taken in the right context, globalization can be a very empowering force. It can bring many new opportunities to entrepreneurs seeking to provide new services, and it can bring new benefits to companies that want to seek out new marketplaces. However, globalization means that you can no longer look out your office window and say, "I am master of all I see." That is too limiting. To succeed in this globalized marketplace, you must master all that you do not see. You must be as open to partnering with a company in New Delhi as you are with a company on Main Street. In fact, you must compete on a global basis if you are to survive and take advantage of all the competitive benefits globalization has to offer.

The only way to stay afloat in a globalized economy is to focus on your core processes and outsource the non-core ones elsewhere. And to get the best quality and least expensive outsourced services, it has become necessary to look outside of your own backyard.

DON'T LOSE SIGHT OF YOUR CUSTOMERS

There's no question that if it's done right, outsourcing the customer service function can bring tremendous benefits in terms of improved service and reduced expenses. However, it's important not to lose sight of your own customers and throw the baby out with the bathwater.

If there's any one thing to watch out for when considering outsourcing customer service, it's the undesired side effect of "customer disconnect." When a third party becomes your customer's first point of contact, you risk losing out on things like customer feedback. "Know your customer" has always been an important part of business. Keep this in mind when negotiating your outsourcing contract.

In other words, you still want to be able to learn from your customers, even when your customers are communicating to you through a third party. When organizing your outsourcing initiative, a good strategy is to retain the ability to track and utilize important metrics that come from customer interaction. You should be able to receive regular, detailed reports from your outsourcer, detailing the type of calls that are received and in what percentages, any customer feedback (positive or negative), and metrics that indicate general customer satisfaction levels.

If you do lose sight of your customers, your success as a company will soon be a thing of the past. While it's easy to keep track of sales metrics, things like satisfaction level are more difficult to track, and if you are outsourcing the customer service function, they are even more difficult to measure. Getting regular feedback on customer satisfaction must be an important element of any outsourcing contract.

When customers call in, they have something specific on their minds. They want to place an order, they want to know how to make something work, or they want to find a particular bit of information. But, in the course of asking for that information, customers, being social creatures, will talk. They may talk about how they appreciate a certain feature or how they dislike another. Those comments aren't directly relevant to fulfilling the customer's primary request, but they are important, nonetheless. The risk of outsourcing is that the third party will take care of all of the primary requests but dismiss the rest as idle chatter. When that happens, you've lost sight of your customer. It's that idle chatter that often gives you insight into problems that you may be unaware of or opportunities for new products or features you haven't yet considered.

When organizing an outsourcing initiative, make sure to understand how that outsourcer manages the entire customer experience. Besides fulfilling the primary customer request, the outsourcer should also:

- Gain an understanding of why customers may stay or leave.

- Keep track of complaints.

- Keep track of praise and positive feedback.

- Keep track of suggestions ("I wish your product had this feature...").

All of the above should be conveyed to you regularly, along

with the routine reports, metrics, order processing data, and other relevant material.

SERVICE LEVEL AGREEMENT

Any type of outsourcing arrangement must come with a service level agreement (SLA). This is a very specific document that can be negotiated, so don't automatically accept and sign your subcontractor's SLA without considering it carefully first.

The basic idea is that the SLA gives you some basic level of assurance from your provider that you will receive the services you contracted for, and that a basic level of quality will be maintained. Even the most basic SLA will include:

- Specific performance levels to be maintained.

- A provision for penalties when service levels are not met.

- Uptime—a guarantee that the outsourced call center will be available and operational, for example, at least 99.9 percent of the time.

- Response time—specific directives on the contractor's response time to your customers as well as response time to you in terms of delivering promised reports.

The SLA itself is an excellent means of starting and maintaining regular communication between you and your contractor. It sets out expectations, as well as provisions for regular contact over the duration of the arrangement. It's extremely useful as a safeguard against escalating costs as well as guaranteeing a level of service.

If you are a small company and your outsourcer is a large one, chances are they will offer you a standard SLA created by their legal department, designed for the most part to serve the contractor's needs best. Don't assume that because you are a small company that the terms of the SLA are not negotiable; in many cases they are. Look over the SLA carefully and make sure that it meets all of your needs. When creating an SLA, consider the following steps:

1. **Create an SLA team.** This team will consist of representatives from your company and your contractor. This is where any negotiation will occur, so members of the team should be very knowledgeable about the business processes being outsourced.

2. **Create and modify the SLA.** This is where you get specific on the details of what is to be provided, what levels of quality are expected, prices, accuracy levels, performance levels, and so forth. Details should be specific. Subjective clauses such as "Contractor will provide reliable service" don't serve any purpose. Instead, say "Contractor will provide service such that no customer will have to wait more than 'X' minutes on hold."

3. **Define responsibilities.** This is where you specify all the various functions, and tasks, including regular management reports that are to be created by the contractor and delivered to you.

4. **Corrective action.** Put teeth into the agreement. Whenever any clause of the agreement is not met—for

example, if the contractor regularly keeps customers on hold longer than the specified period — there must be a penalty or corrective action.

5. **Renegotiation clause.** Over time, the requirements may change, volume may increase or decrease, or the company may desire a higher level of service to be delivered. A clause to renegotiate the terms of the SLA should be in place to accommodate changes in expectations.

In general, the SLA requires both parties to set their requirements and expectations in writing, so both parties understand each other clearly. In addition, it forces both parties involved to consider how the business may grow or change over the duration of a contract, and provisions must be made for that as well. The company's business volume may significantly increase or decrease over the duration of the contract period, and it must be planned for.

Also for the protection of the subcontractor, a clause governing increasing expectations should be included; this guards against an incorrect assumption on the part of the company that the contractor's service levels should improve over time without additional compensation. Some SLAs include clauses that provide for different rates for different levels of service. It may well be possible that responding to customer calls within a minute is substantially more costly to do than responding within two minutes; setting this out in writing will give the company more options.

Gifts.com

Shopping for birthday, Christmas, Valentine's, or other types of gifts can be a lot of fun, but there are some people who it's just impossible to buy for. Whatever they like, they already have, and if there's anything else they're interested in, they're not telling. So what do you do? Socks? Another necktie? A waffle iron? Probably not a great idea, especially if you're trying to be romantic. Gifts.com, launched in March of 2005, has the answer for you.

Gifts.com is a free service that gives online shoppers a set of personalized tools for gift shopping. More than just a catalog, you can also turn to Gifts.com to get good ideas for that hard-to-buy-for person in your life. Gifts.com doesn't sell things directly. Rather, they search through the Web's best online stores to hand-pick the best gifts they can find. You can tell them about your gift recipient and they'll give you some hand-selected ideas for presents. They will also send reminders for special occasions.

Tom Nguyen, Gifts.com Director of Marketing, notes that in the gift-giving business, customer service has to take priority. In addition to a detailed online FAQ, Nguyen and his staff respond to all inquiries, regardless of whether they come in via e-mail or telephone, within 24 hours. "We don't sell any of the products on our site directly," says Nguyen. "Customers buy them from our merchant partners, but we often get inquiries about order status, refunds, etc. One of our objectives is to explain our role in the purchase process clearly on our Web site and provide a mechanism for customers to contact the merchant they purchased from."

Gifts.com is unique in the online shopping world. "We're a new kind of Web site and do not have many direct competitors," said Nguyen. Since they do not sell directly, they don't get a lot of direct queries from customers, but when they do, they are always quick to respond. "We view issues customers have as invaluable feedback about the job that we are doing." The biggest part of customer service for Gifts.com is providing an easy-to-use service that is feature-rich and useful.

"We offer several registered user features to help our customers be better gifters," added Nguyen. "We focus on making our Web site easy to use and fun."

In the classic movie "Miracle on 34th Street," the real Santa Claus causes a bit of a stir while working as a department store Santa at Macy's, and tells a mom to go across the street to Gimbel's to find a toy they didn't have in stock. Gifts.com is a little bit like the Santa character in that movie. Gifts.com's focus on usefulness and customer service is strong. Although you can find a wide variety of special gifts on their site, "from time to time customers may ask about a product we do not feature on Gifts.com," said Nguyen. "We do not hesitate to tell them where they can find what they are looking for if we have this information."

10 CUSTOMER SERVICE TECHNOLOGY

Customer service technology can either improve or destroy the customer experience. Customer service technology includes things like screen pops, which is a type of program that can tell who is calling before the agent answers the phone. The program then delivers a screen to the agent's computer, detailing the caller's order history and other valuable information.

But it doesn't end there. There are dozens, if not hundreds, of customer service software tools available, and some companies spend millions of dollars on them. If you're a smaller company, though, fear not, there are still tools for you that won't break the bank.

Keep in mind, though, that customer service requirements are constantly changing and are very complex, and there is no single product that can offer it all.

AVAILABLE CUSTOMER SERVICE TECHNOLOGIES

The most basic type of customer service technology is the ordinary database. It doesn't even have to be a database specifically created for customer service. It can be something as simple as a spreadsheet or even a box of index cards.

The point is to keep track of customer information. Simple database tools will help you track information such as:

- **Customer contact information.** This is, of course, essential for your marketing efforts as well as your customer service efforts. Keeping track of e-mail addresses, physical addresses, and phone numbers will be useful when orchestrating your next marketing campaign.

- **Customer demographics.** As part of that, you will also want to keep track of some basic demographics, such as age, sex, location, and so forth, so you can further refine your target market.

- **Purchase records.** Keeping track of purchases over time will help you "know" each customer better.

- **Problem resolution.** Track any problems that come up, what they were, and how they were resolved. This will help you serve other customers in the future who may experience similar problems. Also, by looking at a problem log, you may be able to spot some flaws or areas for improvement in your product line.

E-COMMERCE PRODUCTS

Although not primarily considered a customer service tool, your e-commerce platform is indeed a large part of your customer service environment. E-commerce products, for the most part, provide a self-service environment for customer interaction, which lets customers not only make purchases, but learn about your products, compare them with other offerings, and determine whether any additional products being offered will be required (cross-sell). How well and how easily your customers are able to interact with your e-commerce platform is the first thing to consider in customer service.

Your e-commerce platform should provide easy merchandising capability, a shopping cart program that is easy to use, and security for credit card transactions.

Customer service starts with making it easy for them to buy from you. Your e-commerce platform must be straightforward, and your Web site must be easy to navigate.

SEARCH/KNOWLEDGE MANAGEMENT PRODUCTS

Your Web site or electronic catalog contains a vast amount of information, or it should at least. Besides the list of products you have to offer, it should also contain detailed specifications, information on compatibility, installation instructions, and informative articles relating to the use of the products. With potentially thousands of pages available, you need to give your customers an easy way to navigate through it all and find what they are looking for. Before customers make a purchase, they explore information. Giving them the ability to do so on a self-serve basis is the key to good service and better sales. At the very least, include a simple "search" box to allow customers to enter a simple text string to search the contents of your site.

CUSTOMER RELATIONSHIP MANAGEMENT

Early CRM implementations focused almost exclusively on servicing huge companies and were very well known for being large and expensive failures. Today's CRM systems are more successful and can accommodate both large and small implementations.

However, this has come at the expense of an industry shakeout. The options are fewer, with large CRM vendors either buying out the smaller ones or just putting them out of business. This isn't all bad, as it has served the purpose of eliminating the weak players and causing the stronger ones to refine their products to better accommodate the needs of their own customers and create CRM products that really work.

The top CRM vendors include Siebel Systems, Oracle, PeopleSoft, and AmDocs, but there are still some smaller players out there with good solutions. Choosing a CRM suite is a long-term solution. It means a lot more than installing a piece of software. CRM means implementing new business processes, changing the way your departments think about sharing information and cooperating, and, in most cases, spending a tremendous amount of money.

Yet CRM continues to dissatisfy corporate users. In August 2005, Forrester Research estimated that $13 billion was spent on CRM around the world in 2005. Costs include licensing, hardware, software integration, maintenance, and new administration expenses involved in managing these new systems. Forrester discovered that many CRM users are dissatisfied in several areas and want better integration, a better and faster return on investment, and more vendor support. Forrester found that only 29 percent of those surveyed are satisfied with the integration of their CRM systems with existing applications and data sources, 34 percent are satisfied with the vendor interaction post-purchase, and less than half are satisfied that the CRM implementation met their expectations.

Some CRM suites attempt to provide you with everything imaginable; to be a one-stop-shop for creating and maintaining your customer service architecture. In general, it's not possible, but these suites do often contain many useful modules that encompass many of the categories mentioned here. Some even have e-commerce modules.

CUSTOMER PORTALS

Customers always like it when you make it easy for them to do business with you. Of course, they want good prices, quality products, and they want you to have what they need in stock, but if the whole experience is just too difficult or time consuming, they'll go somewhere else.

Customer portals are one tool that helps to make the customer experience convenient and easy to manage. The customer portal is a perfect way to manage the entire end-to-end relationship with your customers; the entire customer lifecycle, if you will.

The portal puts everything they need in one place to maintain or upgrade their equipment, replace products, or buy new ones. The basic idea of the portal is that whenever customers visit your Web site, they log in with a password and are then presented with a custom screen that greets them by name, reminds them when they need to renew something, and makes suggestions for products they are likely to want. Portals can also be used to give customers conveniences like the ability to check their accounts, check on the status of a shipment, or check on whether or not you have a particular product in stock.

A good portal strategy can deliver excellent added value to your customers, while at the same time increasing your sales and reducing your customer service infrastructure costs as a whole. A perfect portal is created from the customer's point of view. It provides the features they want, access to the information they want, and is targeted specifically for each individual user. In short, the portal makes it easier for your customer to do business with you.

When designing your portal, make it a sort of workspace that contains multiple scenarios the customer may desire. Let a customer click on a box that says, for example, "Check my account status," or "Check delivery status." It's a completely customer-focused environment, and it's meant to support the customer's needs.

SERVICE RESOLUTION MANAGEMENT

These customer support software tools focus on the problem-solution phase of customer support. Ideally, this system will allow for a multi-tiered approach, which starts out with a self-service system where customers can diagnose and resolve simple problems on their own without assistance; assisted channels can be brought into the mix later if necessary. A basic service for customers here is the online problem-resolution database, which lists a collection of common problems, along with their resolutions. The list of problems should be maintained constantly and should grow over time. As new problems arise, they can be entered into this database. The idea is that if a problem is not present in the online database and the customer requires human assistance, the resolution will be entered into the database after the interaction takes place, so the next time the problem comes up, human interaction is less likely to be required.

IVR SYSTEMS

An interactive voice response (IVR) system is a type of telephony technology that allows a customer to interact with an automated database that uses voice recognition. It's often used to guide customers to the right department or allow them to access information online. The alternative is to require customers to navigate through a phone menu with a keypad, something that people sometimes find annoying and impersonal. The best IVR systems will allow customers to use natural language commands to navigate and select answers to their questions. It can also be useful in allowing customers to access databases that are also available online, such as shipping status.

SALES FORCE AUTOMATION

Sales force automation (SFA) software isn't traditionally thought of as part of the realm of customer service, but, in reality, customer service should always be a part of sales. Integration between the sales staff and the support staff is a must.

A good sales force automation software package does a lot more than keep track of sales leads. It should be able to help you forecast sales and pipelines, and it should empower your sales staff with information that will help them to better understand their customers, their needs, and their concerns. Customer service begins with the sales staff. It should also provide the sales staff with a 360 degree view of the customer — which means being able to see all of their needs, as well as records such as past purchases, frequency of purchases, preferences, and any problem/resolution scenarios that have come up in the past.

Forecasting is, in reality, a very important part of customer service, and the sales force automation software is where this happens. This functionality gives the sales staff real-time visibility into what each customer's short-term and long-term needs are likely to be, what opportunities may exist for cross-sell and up-sell, and may even be able to keep track of customer inventory to tell when it's time to ask for a new order.

E-SERVICE

A great deal of customer service takes place online, through a combination of FAQs, knowledge bases, e-mail response, call-back buttons and real-time chat. This doesn't mean that phone contact should be eliminated, but providing these channels in an integrated fashion will take a lot of the pressure off of the phone center — allowing the live agents to handle the more difficult calls while the routine inquiries are answered largely on a self-service basis online — and significantly reducing your costs.

Don't make the mistake of relegating your e-service to the back burner, though; inquiries that come in online should be given equal priority to phone inquiries. Ideally, an e-service package will incorporate all of these online features in a single package, as well as case management, reporting, and maintenance of customer histories.

THE BLOG MONSTER

A Web log, or "blog," is a type of informal electronic journal. When they first started appearing, they were largely irreverent rants put out by individuals with various axes to grind, but they have taken a distinctly more commercial use as of late. Corporations are using them to their own advantage to gain insight into their customer base and to find out what's working and what's not and what the customer really wants.

Companies have long used focus groups, customer surveys and polls to get a handle on the customers' wants and needs, in an attempt to improve service levels to the customer. The blog is a natural extension of that and can be much more effective.

In fact, delivering good customer service revolves around "knowing your customer." There are a lot of ways to get to know your customer, but there is always a little bit of a "fudge factor" in company-sponsored polls and focus groups. Focus groups are great, and you'll get some wonderful ideas on how to serve the customer there, but when you're hosting a focus group, you're pampering the customer a bit. You're treating them extra nice by feeding them a nice meal, perhaps giving them a financial incentive to participate—so at that moment, they will probably think more of you and your company than they normally would. When customers are talking about you in a blog, they can let down their guard completely. You get the honest, no-holds-barred viewpoint. This is where you'll really hear about the time the customer went into your store and the clerk ignored him.

Here's an idea of how powerful these little informal diaries are: According to the Pew Internet & American Life Project, 27 percent of Internet users surveyed read blogs, and 7 percent have created one themselves. The interactive nature of blogs has also caught on, with 12 percent of users posting comments or other material on existing blogs.

Part of your information-gathering effort should be to constantly monitor blogs, chat rooms, and newsgroups that may relate to your company and your industry.

There's another side to the blog equation, though: Blogging is not just something individuals do; companies are getting in on the act as well. Besides listening to what customers are saying on blogs, more companies are creating their own corporate blogs as an effective way to disseminate information to the public and elicit feedback from them. According to a survey from Guidewire Group and corporate blogging provider iUpload, corporations are using blogs for both internal and external communications to improve customer relations, as well as their overall business processes. Corporate blogging is a trend that can't be ignored: It will be a major driver in the adoption of social media in years to come. According to the Guidewire survey, corporations of all sizes throughout all industries are using the technology, and 89 percent of respondents are either blogging now or are planning to do so in the future.

E-MAIL CUSTOMER SERVICE

According to a white paper from CRM vendor RightNow Technologies, 41 percent of companies ignored customer e-mails, and only 39 percent responded to customer e-mail inquiries within 24 hours. Another study showed that among the 100 largest U.S. companies, a shocking 12 percent did not respond to online inquiries, 21 percent responded to only half of the inquiries, and 19 percent of responses took four days or more.

Does this make sense? We try to get our telephone hold times down, and we know that customers get upset if they have to stay on hold for more than a minute or two. So why should we make them wait for days to get a response via e-mail? The people who inquire by e-mail are no less important and no less valuable than the ones who inquire by phone, so they should receive the same courteous and fast responses.

Neglecting the e-mail customer service channel can have serious consequences. Besides the risk of losing customers altogether, slow e-mail response defeats the purpose of having e-mail service at all because it drives customers back to the more expensive, phone-based live agent call center.

Customer service inquiries via e-mail are on the increase, as more customers get online and seek it out as a way to save time. Providing inadequate service through this channel may ultimately contribute to losing your competitive edge.

While ordinary e-mail client software does have some basic features for e-mail management, when using e-mail in a customer service environment, you need a little more than the basics. You should be using an e-mail management system that integrates with a customer history and a full view of all relevant customer data. Tracking is another useful feature not found in ordinary e-mail clients. An e-mail management system will assign a ticket number to each message so all customer inquiries can be tracked, logged, and managed — to make sure every problem gets resolved and every question gets answered.

In addition, this sort of system should be able to route e-mail traffic electronically. It will scan messages and automatically evaluate content, and then trigger an action. Some messages may be able to be handled with an automatic "canned" response, while others may be routed to an agent for a more individualized response. The analysis will also be able to route each message to the most appropriate agent.

THE WEB-ENABLED CONTACT CENTER

It goes without saying that the Internet and the Web should be a central focus of your customer service strategy. Chances are at least half of your customers use it, and many of your customers will turn to the Web to try to find an answer to their question before placing a live call. It saves you money and time, and gives the customer a great convenience. When a customer finds an answer to a problem on your Web site, there is no incremental cost for that interaction. When a customer contacts your call center, the incremental cost can be significant, often $20 a call or more.

But creating a Web-enabled contact center requires a lot more than an Internet connection and some software. It requires careful planning and adherence to best practices. CRM solutions provider RightNow Technologies has compiled a list of best practices for the Web-enabled contact center:

1. Having a "champion" take ownership of the web service channel.

2. Make it easy for CSRs to generate new online self-service content.

3. Ensure buy-in for essential collaboration across multiple departments.

4. Commit to continuous improvement of content and processes.

5. Give customers access to service-related content with a single mouse-click.

6. Guide customers to service content before they use the phone or e-mail.

7. Make all useful information on the site available from within the service area.

8. Use graphical and/or interactive material wherever possible.

9. Add as many links across the site as necessary to service/support content.

10. Promote the web channel on "hold" messages and during phone calls.

11. Always provide the ability to speak or chat with a live operator.

12. Auto-suggest answers to customer e-mail inquiries before they're sent to CSRs.

13. Take full advantage of reports and feedback mechanisms to improve content.

14. Activate appropriate escalation/workflow rules.

15. Leveraging knowledge items to speed phone, e-mail and chat responses.

16. Incorporating the web into a total multi-channel contact center strategy.

17. Get started now.

Excerpted from "Best practices for the Web-enabled contact center."
Reprinted with permission, RightNow Technologies, Inc.

TRANSPARENCY AND COMPATIBILITY

A common drawback to many of the customer service tools

you will find is that they all use their own silos of customer and product data. Even the major CRM suites use their own database, and the result is that you will have multiple customer-facing applications, each with its own database, and there is likely to be a high degree of incompatibility.

There's no easy solution, but data integration and data synchronization is an absolute must for a customer service architecture of any size. Operational data stores (ODS) are one approach, which is fed by each application to provide a core repository of data.

One of the greatest things technology can accomplish is to provide transparency to the customer. The customer should not have to see your company as a lot of little, individual departments, each with their own procedures, but rather as a unified whole. Technology should be an enabler. It must be able to allow any person in any department to service every customer's need.

Here's an example: You started to place an order on a company's Web site, but for some reason, the order-taking function doesn't work. You're not sure if it was something wrong with your computer or with the company's server, but the end result is that you couldn't complete your transaction. You then call the company's toll-free number, expecting to have to supply all of the information verbally that you already entered into the dialog box. When the support person answers, and you explain the situation, he asks for your e-mail address. He is immediately able to go into the online order database and see the dropped transaction. He reads back to you all of the information to confirm and completes the transaction for you without delay. The call center and the online order center are two completely different departments with different databases and different servers, but the customer doesn't know that and doesn't particularly care. Because the company has taken the trouble to integrate those two systems and provide transparent access between departments, the customer has been better serviced.

Now that's the way to run a business. A company without transparency would not have the connection between the call center and the online order database, and this would not be able to happen. The customer would have been dissatisfied, or at least inconvenienced, at having to repeat the order over the phone.

The fact is when customers call in, they see the person they are talking to as "the company." They don't realize, or don't care, that the agent on the phone is in one or another department, and they don't stop to think that the agent may or may not have access to certain data. When customers make that call, they think to themselves, *I'm going to call the company.* They don't think *I'm going to call a guy in this company's service department.* When your agents are on the phone, they are "the company." They represent not only their own department, but the entire company, from beginning to end. They're expected to know about the entire operation, have all the answers, and be able to accommodate all of their needs.

SENDING AN E-MAIL TO A CUSTOMER

An unfortunate tendency of the wired world has been to make

e-mails overly informal and often terse. Our responses to e-mails are often not carefully thought out, seldom proofread, and sometimes confusing. When responding to a customer via e-mail, care must be taken to respond in the same professional and clear manner you would if you were writing a letter on paper or interacting in person.

The tendency of e-mail writers is, unhappily, to be "quick and dirty." E-mails are banged out in less than a minute, without any thought or consideration, without adherence to any niceties, and often without any proofreading. We're in a hurry. We want to get the response out of the way. And for some reason, we think it's okay to send a customer a poorly written e-mail, even when we wouldn't consider being as lax in a typewritten response. A sloppy e-mail shows that you have no consideration for your customer, and it creates a bad impression — and in customer service, impression is everything. You represent the company when you are sending a customer an e-mail, and you must maintain a professional image.

Remember, when you are interacting with a customer, whether it is via e-mail or not, it is a formal type of interaction. You are not e-mailing your buddy to confirm your Friday lunch. We've gotten used to using emoticons, abbreviations, and other shortcuts in e-mails, which can make them confusing at times. Some people have the unfortunate tendency to type in all caps when sending an e-mail, which is the equivalent of shouting. These informalities may be fine for personal e-mails, but not when interacting with a customer. Treat e-mail as a professional interaction and adhere to standard professional letter-writing protocol. Greet the person by name (Dear Mr. Smith), state the purpose of the mail, provide the information that is required, and sign off with your full name, title, and contact information.

E-mails too often just jump right into the issue without any greeting or nicety. It makes the e-mail seem terse and impersonal. Make customers feel like they are getting a personal response, by addressing them by name.

Here's a list of common e-mail best practices to use when corresponding with customers:

- Don't use abbreviations or emoticons. They can be confusing and are too informal for customer interaction.

- Greet the customer by name, as you would in a letter.

- Sign off as you would in a letter, with your name, title, and contact information.

- Don't be in a hurry. E-mail is a fast way of communicating, but don't get in too much of a rush here — take time to proofread your e-mail before sending, and carefully think out your response.

- If at all possible, avoid sending large attachments; not everybody has broadband.

- Always include a descriptive subject line to catch your customer's attention right away, so your response won't get mistaken for an advertisement or spam (for example, "Response to your query on product availability").

- Respond in a timely manner.

- Recognize when a situation requires you to go offline and give a personal response via telephone or face-to-face contact.

E-mail management also becomes an issue in the customer service realm. As with any customer communication, e-mail correspondence should be logged and archived.

CREATING CUSTOMER SERVICE IN AN ONLINE ENVIRONMENT

D o you dotcom? Is your business and your customer contact completely virtual? You're not alone. A common factor in the failure of online businesses is the lack of real customer service, and the unfortunate tendency of online entrepreneurs to automate to the point of eliminating any sort of in-person contact. But in reality, your dotcom isn't just an ATM machine attached to your computer, there are real people out there buying your product, and you must interface with them.

Ultimately, the key to successful online customer service is putting a human face on it. Online customer service should be just as personalized as when you deliver face-to-face customer service, and with the available technology today, it's easy to offer that level of personalization. Even though customers may be interacting online, they still must get the feeling that they are interacting with humans. Avoid the temptation to create a Web site that is so completely automated and impersonal that customers walk away feeling that they have been serviced by a robot.

When establishing your online customer service center, one thing to keep in mind is that your online service center is not your only service center—or at least it shouldn't be. Customers should have at their disposal as many different avenues of being serviced as you can provide, including:

- E-mail support

- Telephone support

- Fax-back

- Real-time IM chat

- Walk-in service center

- Proactive support—you contact them before they have to contact you

One of the most vitally important things about establishing your online service functions is to realize that these functions should be given the same priority as any other method. There's no reason a customer sending you an e-mail should have to wait two or three days to get a response, while someone calling into your toll-free number can get a problem resolved immediately.

A WEB SITE ISN'T AN EXCUSE TO HIDE THE HUMANS

During the dotcom boom of the late eighties and early nineties, a lot of dotcoms came into being, made a lot of noise, and then died out. Only a very small percentage of them are still around today. There are several reasons why they died out, but one of them is this: They took the miracle of the Internet too far. True enough, the Internet revolution introduced a new paradigm to the business world. It brought us new tools and techniques, and it created a new set of expectations. It generated new business opportunities, while making others obsolete.

Those dotcoms that failed made the mistake of thinking that a business could be entirely automated. Early online stores were completely impersonal, and the ideal of those early dotcommers was to create a business that was so entirely automated and online that it could run itself. We have learned since then, however, that regardless of the level of automation that is available, there is no such thing as a business that runs itself.

Statistics bear out the fact that online shopping venues are gaining a bigger piece of the shopping pie. Online shopping makes it easy to compare prices, it's faster and more expedient, and usually results in some cost savings. For the most part, although security vulnerabilities still persist, online shopping is fairly reliable and safe as long as consumers observe good security practices and don't fall prey to scams, social engineering, and other tricks to try to get your account numbers. But still, it's not going to replace brick-and-mortar shopping completely. Why? One reason: Online shopping is functional; going to a store is social.

Think about it: Much as we may complain about the crowds during the holidays, it's still a fun experience to go downtown, browse through all the stores, sit in a coffeehouse for a while and watch people go by, look at the lights, and maybe see a group of carolers strolling down the street in costume. Online shopping takes the fun and social element out of shopping, transforming it into a lonely, solitary function. Sure, we get the satisfaction of saving time and money, but we miss out on the experience.

That said, online shopping has its place; it's growing, and merchants must embrace it in order to succeed in the coming years. But in so doing, merchants must also serve their online customers by putting some humanity back into the online shopping experience. You must reinforce to your customers that there are actual, live people behind that Web site. Here are a few tips on how to accomplish this:

- **Make the Web site more usable.** Remember, your online customer is all alone out there, with nobody to explain how your shopping cart works. Make it easy to use and self-explanatory.

- **Make your Web site festive and fun.** It should be more than just functional; it should be attractive to look at, entertaining, and informative.

- **Include cross-channel support.** Many shoppers use the Web for doing research before buying a product at a physical store. Make a connection between your Web site and your physical storefront to encourage this.

- **Include a facility for live support.** Your Web site isn't a robot; it's just an electronic portal to your business. Include a toll-free number, e-mail address for e-mail support, live chat facility, fax-back, or as many ways as you can support to allow the customer to get additional information or talk to a live agent.

CREATING A CUSTOMER-FRIENDLY SITE

According to Forrester Research, companies tend to be a lot better at supporting brand positioning than they are providing usability for their customers. The PR and advertising people will do a wonderful job of brand positioning, making sure that the site features logos prominently and reinforces the company brand on each page, but that does nothing to make the site easy to use for the customer. And in the end, without usability, any exercises in branding are useless, because the customer will abandon the site out of frustration. While image and brand are all very important concepts, building a Web site must first take into account usability — what your visitors want and how they find it — before turning it over to the marketing team.

Creating a customer-friendly Web site is an important part of servicing your customers and providing them with a friendly environment. This is important whether or not yours is an online-only or brick-and-mortar business. If you have a storefront, you wouldn't think of taking a series of items for sale and displaying them in the broom closet, would you? Of course not. You want to make every single item in your store easy to get to and easy to see. You don't want your customers to have to work too hard to find what they want, because, in fact, customers aren't willing to go to a great deal of trouble. If they don't see it within the first few minutes, chances are they will walk out of the store and go somewhere else.

Unfortunately, a lot of Web sites place products in the virtual equivalent of a broom closet. The greatest disservice a Web designer can give a customer is having a site with too many layers. No customer should ever have to click more than two or three times to get to where they want to go once they visit your home page. Yet, some of the biggest companies around still create enormously complex Web sites with seemingly endless menus. Here's an example of two Web sites, both selling women's fashions. A visitor comes to the home page, looking for a pair of earrings. The first series of clicks goes something like this:

- Home page

- Fashions

- Apparel

- Accessories

- Jewelry

- Earrings

The harried shopper must click five times after landing on the home page before finding the earrings page. On the other hand, a well-designed Web site with the same products is organized something like this:

- Home page

- Jewelry

- Earrings

Only two clicks! The design is flatter, with more selections in each level, but still manageable. The shopper doesn't have to hunt for her earrings, and the virtual store owner is a lot more likely to make the sale because the shopper won't abandon the search before the item is found.

Some other elements of customer-friendly design include:

- **Make your site easy to navigate.** Your customers should be able to tell at a glance, right from your home page, where they need to go to find what they want. Nobody should have to hunt for anything on your Web site.

- **Make it easy for your customers to contact you live.** Include a "Contact us" click box on every page, with an immediate link to a page with your toll-free number, e-mail address, and chat-back details if you have it.

- **Resist the urge to use significant amounts of bandwidth-intense animation and graphics**, no matter how cool it looks when your Webmaster shows it to you. Not all people have broadband, and faced with the prospect of having to wait for a Flash animation to load, most customers without a high-speed connection will just move on to the next site.

A customer-friendly site is also one that is dynamic. Some brick-and-mortar businesses simply put up a basic Web site with the virtual equivalent of a brochure or flyer, describing the basics of the company's products or services and listing a contact number. That's simply not enough. Having a site with dynamic, constantly changing and always fresh information will keep your customers interested and keep them coming back to your Web site. This is what's known in the trade as a "sticky" Web site—one that has the ability to keep customers coming back.

Some examples of how to create a "sticky" Web site include:

- Creating a weekly or monthly newsletter relating to the use of your products.

- Installing a customer discussion board or forum.

- Running contests online.

- Offering free services such as virtual greeting cards or screen savers that can be downloaded from your site.

And, as always, just keep the site looking good. A good Web site will be designed by a professional. Your Web site is a key part of your business, and its development should not be relegated to an amateur.

Lastly, making a customer-friendly site means having a customer-friendly address. When you create a physical store, you want to make it easy to understand where it is. You may, for example, advertise your store's address and add a line that says something like, "Downtown, just east of Main Street," to make it very clear where your store is located. Your URL is your virtual address. Make it easy to remember, straightforward, and free of unusual characters and long text strings. Let's take a fictional store called Bob's Phone Shop. Which of the two addresses will you be able to remember ten minutes from now?

- **www.bobsphoneshop.com**

- **www.freesites.com/portal/?/Bob/Homepage /CustNo98765.html**

Spending a few dollars to buy your own domain will make it easier for customers to remember where you are in cyberspace. Using the free hosting sites is unprofessional and usually forces you to use long URLs that are difficult to remember.

YOUR SEARCH STRATEGY

Your customers need to be able to find you, and once they do, they need to be able to find what they're looking for.

The Web is a big place. Imagine, for example, that you are looking for one very specific item, and you walk into the biggest mall in the world to try to find it. There are a thousand stores, but only one carries what you want. It would be a little overwhelming. Without search functionality, the Web would be a little like that.

A basic element of providing good customer service is making your customers' shopping experience easy and pleasant, not confusing. It may be something as simple as laying out your goods in a logical order to make it easier for visitors to your physical store, or organizing your Web site with an opening screen that includes a menu that divides your goods into certain logical categories. It's a simple and straightforward tenet of service: If your customers can't find what they want, they won't come back.

In the online world, this means using search technology in two different ways: First, you must have what some are referring to as a "Google strategy" to facilitate external searches; second, you must build your own Web site so that customers can find what they want through a combination of good design and a site-based search facility.

There are, of course, multiple search engines, but Google is by far the biggest and most prominent, and the word "Google" has come to have a generic usage, as in, "Google that for me and see what you can find out." Your Google strategy is simply a plan of action to help your customers find out where you are in cyberspace.

In cyberspace, if you build it, they will not come. The millions of dotcom stores that have failed found out rather quickly that it's simply not possible to create an online store, put it in cyberspace, and wait for people to show up. Cyberspace is like physical real estate, when you open a store, you have to advertise and let people know you are there. You get a listing in the Yellow Pages. You put up a billboard and some flyers. Your company's Google strategist will ensure that your customers can find you easily, through tasks that include:

- Oversee keyword purchase "pay-per-click" advertising.

- Optimize content so that specific keyword searches cause your company to turn up in the first page of "hits."

- Use technology to constantly monitor where your site shows up on various Google keyword searches.

Within the site itself, make your site easy to navigate, and include a search box that lets people do keyword searches within the confines of your site.

E-MAIL ADVERTISING

Everything you do comes down to service, whether it's directly the domain of the customer service department or not. Advertising is especially important in this regard, since your advertisements and your overall ad strategy will set the pace and create an image for your company. The image you want to create is one of service and consideration for your customers.

Online advertising, especially e-mail advertising, is an especially tricky and sensitive area. In the early days of the Internet, there was a contingent of people who didn't want to allow advertising on it at all and took great exception when it started to appear. This is obviously an idealistic and unworkable philosophy. Imagine trying to have a daily newspaper or a television show without advertising. The money to run these things has to come from somewhere, and that somewhere is advertising. Nonetheless, the anti-ad philosophy reared its ugly head in the Internet world, and even though today advertising has become commonplace and a necessary part of anybody's Internet commerce strategy, one must tread these waters carefully.

You can adopt a service-oriented online advertising strategy. It takes a little more work, but in the end, your customer will be better serviced, will know you better, and you will have greater success. First, let's look at what the alternative to a service-oriented online advertising strategy is: It's called spam. Just the mention of the word evokes strong reactions in people.

Unsolicited online e-mail advertisements are not welcome. They tend to make people angry; you don't get many customers from spamming, and you may even lose the ones you already have. Again, it's very different from any other type of advertising. Most advertising is by nature unsolicited. When we watch a television show, our viewing gets interrupted by appeals to buy various goods and services. We didn't ask to see those appeals, but they are there, nonetheless, and we accept them. Similarly, so-called junk mail appears in our mailboxes. During the holidays, we get a mailbox full of gift catalogs, coupons, and shoppers; we look at the ones that seem interesting and throw the rest away. There doesn't seem to be any big move to make it illegal for companies to send catalogs through the U.S. mail. We don't, however, accept unsolicited appeals sent through e-mail. It's an inconsistent attitude, but, nonetheless, it's real and must be respected. The consequences can be devastating. Sending bulk unsolicited e-mail advertisements can have unintended consequences, and regardless of whether you think it's a good idea, the bottom line is that it annoys more people than it will attract. It's not service-oriented. For that reason, it's a poor strategy.

Think of advertising not just as a way to get business; think of it as a way to help people. You want to help them find what they want, to get a good deal, to gather information. Your advertisement is put there for that purpose. In so doing, people will come to your online store.

But if we can't send out unsolicited e-mail advertisements, how do we advertise via e-mail? Do people actually request them? Yes, they do. There are several ways you can get valid e-mail addresses of people who have actually requested ads that promote the type of products you have.

There are several online venues that offer premiums, bonuses, gifts, and other goodies in exchange for demographic information and the right to send e-mail ads. Companies like MyPoints, for example, reward people with "points" for visiting certain merchants and responding to certain ads. Those points can be saved up to purchase goods. In fact, these sorts of programs are much better than unsolicited spam since they are targeted. In other words, the people who join these programs will indicate their interests, and they will receive advertisements that correspond to those interests. One of the most annoying things about spam is getting ads that are simply irrelevant. Targeted programs like these won't be sending e-mail ads for Viagra to 90-year-old ladies (unless they've specifically mentioned an interest, and then that's a story that's none of our business...).

You can also orchestrate a good customer-friendly e-mail advertising campaign by collecting e-mail addresses of existing customers. This is your best audience and the people who are most likely to make purchases. Another way is to offer a subscription-based free newsletter with valuable content and information relevant to your product and your customers' interests.

CREATE A CONTENT-RICH WEB SITE

The world of online commerce has created a whole new set of customer service standards and expectations. Customers now expect to be able to get great deals online; they expect to be able to find them easily and compare prices with other sites; they expect their online experiences to be trouble-free and easy; and they expect to get quality information about your company, your product, your industry, and everything related to it for free.

It's no longer enough to just simply offer a good product. For example, let's say you run a company that sells skateboards. You carry great skateboards and accessories, you sell skateboarding magazines, and offer good prices, but your competitor, who also has a Web site, is getting all the business. *Why?* you think to yourself. Your prices are better. You have a good shopping cart that is functional and easy to use. You don't spam, and you invest in pay-per-click advertising.

Here's the reason: Your competitor, besides having all that, also has a content-rich site. He has valuable, original articles about skateboards, about the sport of skateboarding in general, guides on the best places to skate, and an exclusive interview with Tony Hawk. While you sell skateboarding magazines, your competitor is offering better and fresher content, for free. In fact, good e-commerce is content-driven as much as it is product-driven. The Internet is a place where people turn to for information more than for something to buy; more often than not, the buying is secondary to the information.

When you have a physical store, you service your customers by hiring knowledgeable salespeople who can help them with their decisions and answer their questions. The guy behind the counter at the local skateboard shop knows all the cool spots to skate, and he knows which boards will give the buyer the best wear for the money. He understands that the wheels you purchase to go onto the board will make a big difference and can recommend the best ones for your needs. And he can probably tell an entertaining story or two about being run out of downtown by the cops.

But when you're online, the guy behind the counter isn't there. Providing rich, original content on your site is the next best thing.

THE CHECKOUT PROCESS

Online marketers are always frustrated over the amount of visitors who abandon shopping carts before completing a purchase. There are a number of reasons a visitor starts to make an order using your electronic shopping cart but then does not complete the purchase; these reasons may include:

- **The shopper was using the shopping cart as a way to determine the total price including shipping.** Shipping fees are often not disclosed in advance of the purchase, but only added on to the shopping cart after the items are placed inside.

- **Simple confusion.** The shopping cart application was too complicated.

- **Limited payment options.** Shoppers may find out at the last minute that you do not accept their type of credit card or do not accept mail-in payments.

The key, as always, is flexibility. Offer multiple payment options, keep the design simple, and let them know ahead of time what your shipping fees will be.

A newer and more innovative option is to avoid the virtual

checkout entirely and opt for a live checkout. Companies like InQ and LiveChat provide a live chat utility to supplement the online checkout. Adding a live chat utility to the checkout facility allows your customers to ask last-minute questions while they are completing their purchases. Whenever there is any confusion at checkout time, without a live person facilitating the transaction, the natural tendency of the shopper is simply to abandon the transaction. The live chat functionality will add an extra measure of customer service, providing a real person at the other end of the electronic transaction—so customers can ask about shipping, product options, or anything else they may be confused about.

The live chat utility doesn't have to be limited to the checkout process. Some companies include a live chat link on every page on the site, making it easy for customers to IM with a service agent at any time. Adding the simple instant-messaging functionality between your staff and your customers goes a long way toward adding a "human element" to your Web site. It helps avoid dropped transactions, encourages customers to stay on your site longer, and will ultimately result in more sales because customers feel like they have been truly engaged and catered to in a way that few other online presences can do.

CUSTOMER SELF-SERVICE

The Web is about convenience, and convenience means different things to different people. While some customers do much better talking to a real person, others would prefer to do it themselves, if at all possible. It's up to you to provide them with the tools. Providing self-service as an option services these customers better, and also saves money out of the customer service budget.

Some elements of your online presence that allow customers to serve themselves include:

- **The FAQ,** a list of common questions and answers to common problems.

- **Site search.** A search engine designed to allow customers to search your site for what they are looking for.

- **Configurators.** Sometimes used in environments where customers order custom-made products. This is a piece of software that lets customers design their product online from a range of options, and instantly see the price based on the options they have selected.

- **Electronic shopping cart.** Automates the purchasing and check-out process.

CHAPTER 12

CUSTOMER SERVICE STRATEGIES

THE CALL LOG

When a customer calls in to get service, there's nothing more annoying than having to re-explain a situation each time, often to different individuals. While it's always best if you can provide a single agent to each client, sometimes it's not possible, and people who call in will often end up talking to more than one agent—even if there is one agent that is "in charge" of that account. And even if the customer is lucky enough to get the same person each time, that agent may be managing hundreds of accounts, and it's not always easy to remember everybody's situation.

Nonetheless, you want to make it seem like you do. That's why you maintain a call log. In the old days, it would be a simple handwritten sheet, kept conveniently close to the telephone. After each call, the agent would make notes as to the content of the call, and make notes about anything that had to be done. When the customer would call in again, the agent would be able to quickly grab the right sheet, and tell at a glance what the status of the situation would be at any given time.

Ideally, this sheet would also have a few notes about the client, the nature of the client's account, and a few personal things as well. For example, if the client's name is Stanislaw but he likes to be called "Stash," it should be so noted on the client sheet. It's a small thing, but it makes the call more personal. Make a few other notes too. As an agent talks to a client over time, the agent is likely to glean information like what the client's favorite sports team is, what kind of car he drives, or what he bought his wife for her last birthday. These things may have nothing at all to do with what you sell, but knowing a little bit about your client will make your sales job easier, and it will also help make the customer feel more comfortable with your company.

But besides knowing that Stash is married to Helen and they have three kids, he drives a Lincoln, and likes the Cubs, the call log, of course, contains a variety of necessary information related to problems and resolutions, orders, and requests. It should have a record of every incoming and outgoing call, and a history of transactions.

Today, most call logs are not the pen-and-paper variety, but take the form of "screen pops." These are computer programs that are tied to the phone system, such that as soon as the call comes in, the telephony application determines from caller ID technology who is calling, and automatically places the call log on the computer screen in front of the agent before the phone is even answered. Alternately, you can create call logs on your computer that are a bit less sophisticated, but still allow you to gain very quick access to the customer records and all other relevant information.

THE CUSTOMER SERVICE BLOG

Blogs are highly informal. Blog writers feel like they can "let their hair down" when they are writing, free from restraints that confine us when we are speaking in public. Polite niceties are put aside and people say what they really think here. Monitor blogs that relate to your company or your industry to see what people really think. This will give you a much better idea of the prevailing attitudes out there than any customer survey ever will.

On the other side of the blogging fence, run your own company blog as a way to keep your customers informed about new developments and opportunities.

ATTITUDE AND DEMEANOR

There are a lot of customer service guides that offer a lot of platitudes about maintaining a positive attitude, offering very important-sounding advice about putting a smile on your face while you're on the phone, saying please and thank you, and putting your best foot forward. Most of these things are common sense and should have been taught to us by our mothers by the time we were eight-years-old, so we'll resist the urge to add these types of lists here.

Having said that, however, attitude and state of mind are greatly important to the customer service function. The hiring manager must be able to recognize a "people person," and the agent must be able to truly enjoy talking with and serving others. There are people who come to work every day with a chip on their shoulder, who like to argue, who nitpick over little details, and just don't like to talk to others. These are the people who should work in the back office and away from customers. Part of hiring customer service people is the ability to recognize someone with a good personality, who is capable of carrying on a pleasant conversation, and who is interested in going out of his or her way to solve problems for people.

Sometimes it is difficult to keep this sort of friendly demeanor every day, five days a week, in the face of constant problems and distractions. Even the friendliest and most personable agent of all will have bad days, will get tired of the routine, and occasionally frustrated with the job. Don't expect the agent to be at 100 percent every minute of the day, but do provide the agents with some avenues to help them be there as much as possible. Here are a few ideas you can implement to help your agents be at their best:

- **Customer service agents have to hold in a lot.** They sometimes want to say things that they cannot. They have to deal with unreasonable customers and difficult requests. They may get yelled at or insulted by customers, and they may sometimes have to talk to a customer who just doesn't understand what they are trying to tell them. When agents hold this in for too long, they will burn out. Hold a gripe session once a month. Provide pizza and drinks after hours, and let your agents blow off steam.

- **Learn to recognize signs of stress.** Customer service is often a very stressful job; learn to recognize it in your agents. If you see agents who are ready to blow, take them off task for a while. Send them on errands or let them do another task for a couple hours that doesn't involve talking to anybody.

- Small comforts make the workplace happier and keep your agents on-task. Little things like free gourmet coffee and donuts in the morning, comfortable chairs, and the freedom to decorate their work areas with homey pictures and frills will help keep your agents happy and stress-free.

THINK PROACTIVELY

Much of customer service involves reacting to situations. It may be reassuring customers that their order is being taken care of when the factory floor has experienced some delay. It may call for some hand-holding when the customer has become angry or upset about something, or it may be finding a good alternative to a customer who wants a product that you don't have in stock or don't carry.

But, in fact, customer service also involves thinking ahead. It's not all "putting out fires," but making sure the fires don't happen in the first place. If you feel that a complaint is imminent—if, for example, a customer received the wrong goods, a shipment has been delayed, or you discover that the customer has been disserviced in some way—then the best strategy is to proactively take up the situation and be the first to mention it. In other words, beat the customer to the punch. Don't wait for the complaint to come; instead, acknowledge the problem, apologize for it, and explain what is being done to fix it, before the customer has a chance to complain about it.

Another part of proactive customer service is just knowledge gathering. Through tools such as customer surveys, active listening, and open-ended questions, you can gain a better understanding of what your customers want and need, what they expect, and how you can serve them better. Customers won't always tell you everything that's on their mind, so you won't know until you ask. Gaining a better understanding of that customer will help you to think proactively and avoid problem situations from happening in the first place.

THE CUSTOMER IS ALWAYS RIGHT—UNTIL HE'S WRONG

Yes, we try to please our customers. We go out of our way to accommodate them, make exceptions to policy, and, in general, go the extra mile. We look the other way when they say something offensive and we laugh at their bad jokes, but it can only go so far.

What do you do when the customer is absolutely, positively, dead wrong? When what they are saying simply cannot be justified under any circumstances? When their request is so completely unreasonable there's absolutely no way to justify accommodating it? We hope that such a situation never happens, and, yes, in most cases it's simply good customer service to be accommodating, to look the other way, and go the extra mile to make sure the customer gets the best service you can give and then some. But sometimes, it happens: There will come a day when you have to say no. The best way to do that is, of course, politely, explaining why it cannot be done, and by including an alternative: "I'm sorry, we can't accommodate that. The part you describe would require our machinery to place a square peg into a round hole, and our engineering team advises us that it would create a structural weakness in your end product. They did make up an alternate drawing, though, and I think this concept will work just as well for you. May I show it to you?"

Take note however, that in your explanation, avoid any of the following:

- "It's against policy."

- "We can't do it."

- "It's a bad idea."

- "The boss/engineering crew/service people/whoever says we can't do it."

- "We've never done that before."

Such vagaries are not allowed and would create a disservice to your customer. Be specific.

There are times, however, when even offering a sound explanation and a reasonable alternative isn't enough, and the customer causes more problems than he or she is worth. Such situations are thankfully rare, but they do occur. Sometimes customers are so demanding and unreasonable that servicing them would cost you too much money and would even possibly cause you to disservice other customers in the process. There's only one thing to do in such a situation, and that's to fire the customer.

Firing a client is much like firing an employee; it's not something to be taken lightly, and it must be done carefully and with a great deal of caution and tact. It's often best to put it in writing, and lay out the details in such a way as not to offend the departing client. Even though you may wish to say something like, "You are a pain in the neck. Don't ever come to my shop again," the following is probably a better approach:

> "Over the course of our relationship, we have always valued you as a customer. However, as your business and needs have changed, we feel that we are no longer in a position to accommodate you, and regret that we will no longer be able to serve your company."

Be prepared to take a little flack, but stand firm in your decision.

EMPOWER YOUR CUSTOMER

Empowerment is a critical element all around. We've discussed the need for management to empower their customer service people to make decisions and handle situations as they arise. Customer service staff must also learn the art of empowerment, because clients themselves need to feel empowered.

If you are a customer service agent and you are talking to clients, the natural order is that the customers want you to do something or provide something. That puts you in the power seat, since you have something they want, and they need to get it from you. Often, customers calling in for help feel powerless and like they are not in control. They may be hesitant to make requests or suggestions, and they may feel powerless in the face of a large corporation. The natural tendency of all people is to see corporations as impersonal, policy-driven machines — and if something doesn't fit into policy, then it can't be done. One of the most common complaints about corporations is the "red tape" that one must go through to find out anything or get anything done, especially if it deviates even slightly from the norm. That makes the customer feel helpless.

Eliminating this feeling of helplessness will go a long way toward making your customers feel more secure with you, making them more loyal, and providing better customer service. Here are a few ways to make customers feel like they are in control of the situation:

- **Offer them choices.** Instead of just giving them a single response, explain to them what their various options may be, and the relative pros and cons of each. Instead of just selecting the best option for customers and presenting it to them, let customers decide for themselves, based on your expert guidance.

- **Ask customers for feedback** as you try to solve their problem. Instead of just coming up with a solution, ask them what they think should be done or what they would like to see happen.

- **Explain the details.** Don't assume that customers will understand everything you have to say, especially technical jargon. Talk on their same level, whatever level that may be. Obviously, if your customer is a rocket scientist, you can probably use all the jargon you want; but if your customer is a boutique owner, you may need to offer a bit more explanation about technical products.

A SERVICE GUARANTEE

It's one thing to say that you give superior customer service; it's another thing entirely to back it up with a guarantee. In some industries, a company will offer a "Service Level Agreement," or SLA, which specifically lays out in hard numbers exactly what the customer can expect and what measures will be taken if those promises are not met. In some cases, an SLA may be several pages long and very detailed.

Service guarantees don't necessarily have to be so detailed. The neighborhood pizza restaurant that says "Delivery within 20 minutes or it's free" is making a powerful service guarantee with just seven words. Several different things happen when you make a service guarantee like this. First of all, it reinforces to your customers that you mean business, and it lets them know that they are very likely to get what they have been promised. But secondly, it forces the company to take stock of their internal processes. If you're promising a 24-hour turnaround on all service calls, you have to take a careful look at your processes, your workflow, and your internal procedures to make sure that you can meet that promise at all times. Making these guarantees forces the company, in other words, to continuously refine and improve their internal processes.

Making guarantees like this also forces the company to do a post-analysis when a promise does get broken. Suppose you've promised 24-hour turnaround, but a customer had to wait 30 hours instead. You had to deliver for free. The customer is still happy, but you've lost money. Suppose you are running the pizza restaurant making the "20 minutes or free" guarantee. You analyze the traffic, average delivery times, and how fast your drivers respond, and you determine that 20 minutes is reasonable. But there are no absolutes, and even though your delivery people almost always deliver several minutes under the 20-minute guarantee, things happen. You may get behind in production because the football team just came in and ordered twenty pizzas. There may be a traffic jam. The delivery person may get a flat tire.

Still, after running the program for a while, you realize that you have to deliver a free pizza about once a month. You figure that's a pretty good success rate, and you're happy with it. It costs you the price of a pizza, but on the other hand, it results in significant gains to offset that loss. You get more customers because they know they can get good service on a regular basis. You sell more pizzas than you would otherwise, and the program is a success.

The pizza restaurant down the street, however, wants to beat you at your own game, so they implement a 10-minute guarantee. But that store owner isn't quite as bright as you are, and he doesn't do his research. He offers his 10-minute guarantee and gets an initial rush of business—temporarily taking away some of yours. After a few weeks of this, he realizes that his people aren't able to deliver on that promise. He's giving away too many free pizzas and losing money. Customers are taking advantage because they realize they can watch the clock and have a good shot at getting a free pizza. He will eventually have to renege on the promise, which will cost him big time in terms of goodwill and customer loyalty. When he takes down the 10-minute guarantee sign, customers will no longer have faith in his shop, he will go out of business, and you will once again have cornered the neighborhood pizza market.

The only way to practically offer such guarantees is to be reasonably sure that you won't ever have to make good on them, or if you do, it will be at an acceptably low frequency. The steps involved are:

1. **Crunch the numbers and determine what an acceptable rate of failure would be.** If you miss the mark on one in a thousand, will your losses be acceptable? Of course, you must strive for 100 percent, but at the same time, be aware of your loss rates that may result from making your guarantees.

2. **Re-visit all of your relevant internal processes to make sure that everything is functioning optimally.** Implement a strategy of continuous improvement so that your processes are constantly examined. Be open to improvements in your processes and procedures.

3. **When you fail to meet a guarantee, conduct a post-service session.** Look at the transaction from beginning to end, and determine why, in detail, the failure occurred.

4. **Implement new or revised procedures** to make sure that the failure does not happen again.

Saint Joseph County Public Library

The Saint Joseph County Public Library (SJCPL), located in South Bend, Indiana, has ranked among the top ten public libraries serving populations of between 100,000 and 250,000 in the United States, every year for the past six years. The fourth largest public library in the state, SJCPL consists of a main branch downtown, and seven branch libraries located throughout the county. The library fills several roles in the county, with the primary role being "Information Services Hub for the Community." Serving the public through technology and superior Internet services has always been a part of this role.

In 1994, the library became the very first public library in the United States, and the second in the world, to run its own Web server and place its home page on the Internet. The first to do so, the Public Library of Helsinki, Finland, went live only two weeks before St. Joseph County. Today, SJCPL's Web site is one of the most bookmarked public library sites in the world, with over 12,000 hits a day.

"Customer service means everything to our library," said branch manager Joseph Sipocz. "We are taxpayer-funded and we rely on our reputation in the community to justify our budget." Technology naturally plays a large part in the library's ongoing customer service focus. In St. Joseph County, library patrons have much more than just books on a shelf. "We use technology to offer access," said Sipocz. Library patrons can get access to online databases for magazine articles, health information, business and genealogy research, and much more. "We offer public Internet access to cardholders. We communicate with the community with our Web site and blogs. We have the option of e-mailing hold and overdue notices to the public."

On a typical day, the library is full of patrons searching through online databases, accessing the Internet, and, yes, even looking at books off the shelf. Part of the library's customer service focus is communicating what is available, said Sipocz. "We attract customers through our Web site, through articles in the local newspaper, through contacts with the local television and radio stations, and by being a visible presence in the community."

The library's customer focus is pervasive at all levels. "All of our staff are customer service personnel," added Sipocz. "We look for the ability to work courteously with the public." And part of good customer service is giving the public what they want, something at which SJCPL excels. If you're looking for contemporary, modern fiction, some libraries miss the mark, but not in St. Joseph County. "Unlike some library systems, we order multiple copies of popular materials to coincide with public demand. Some library systems do not purchase popular movies or music, while we do. Generally, we try to offer the public the library materials they want."

In the library, public service is everything. To SJCPL's staff, "it means that our public feels comfortable coming to our libraries, finds the services and materials they want, and are treated with respect by the staff." Customer service is pervasive throughout the library, and management has offered training for customer service and includes superior service in its long-range plans and goals.

And even though it is a taxpayer-supported organization, the library still must focus on retaining its customers through superior service. "We retain customers by putting money into keeping current library collections and through excellent customer service," added Sipocz. And in the rare case of an unsatisfied customer, the library's engaged and empowered staff is always right on top of the situation. "We do what we can to make things right for unsatisfied customers," explained Sipocz. "In the caes of members of the public who wish to censor materials, we can only suggest that others have the right to the materials that they want, just as they do. Or that the parent may restrict what their child reads/views/hears, but only they can decide—we're not their parents. As for problems with fines and overdues, we will sometimes reduce cash owed if we get our materials back. We give clerks some leeway in working with patrons."

CHAPTER

13

OFFICE POLITICS

Customer service can be a pressure-cooker, and every now and then, one of the agents may blow a fuse. Delivering good customer service starts by creating a positive work environment. Unhappy, disgruntled, underpaid and stressed out employees will not be able to service your customers well.

Sure, all the customer service manuals will tell you to check your personal problems at the door. Don't take out your aggressions on the customer. Service with a smile. Turn that frown upside down, and other similar claptrap. Those are all meaningless. The bottom line is: If your customer-facing employee is in a bad mood, the customer will know it, regardless of how many smiley faces and sappy slogans you post on the break room wall.

No matter how much you try to encourage your staff to be nice to the customers, office politics happen. And if your staff is preoccupied with some perceived slight or injustice that happened internally, they will not be operating on all eight cylinders when dealing with customers. Conflicts in the office, incompatible personalities, and endless nitpicking and company politics will almost always result in customers being disserviced, or not serviced to the degree that they should be. There are two things that happen here to disservice customers:

1. **Employees who are feuding will not work together like they should to resolve customer problems and provide adequate service.** Customer service requires a strong level of cooperation, and it's hard for people who don't get along to cooperate.

2. **Employees will be distracted from serving the customer by internal squabbles and office politics.** While the customer-facing employee should be thinking about solving the customers' problem and finding out when their order will be delivered, the employee is instead thinking in the back of his or her mind, *I'm so mad that so-and-so got that promotion; she's such an idiot! She doesn't know what she's doing at all.*

KEEPING A FRIENDLY OFFICE ENVIRONMENT

Have you ever worked in an office? Then you've probably noticed it. The unspoken tension that often exists between workers for one reason or another, the resentment over the hierarchy and who is over whom, and just bad feelings because "that person rubs me the wrong way." And it's not always easy for a supervisor to make everybody in the office play nice together.

What does the work area look like? Human resources people pay a lot of attention to things like the color of the walls, windows and sunlight, and live plants. These things are more than just decorations, they make the office more tolerable — and help keep the staff happy and productive.

Some offices, in a manager's zeal to keep a professional atmosphere, forbid things like pictures and personal decorations on individual cubicles. The office then becomes a sterile and unfriendly place. However, it is these small touches, the pictures of our kids and small decorations that reflect each person's personality, that help to make the office more tolerable. To be sure, there must be rules that govern good taste and offensive items should not be allowed, but individuality in décor should be encouraged. The very nature of office cubicles is to make an office uniform and unfriendly. They are, after all, nothing but small gray boxes containing identical sets of desks and computer terminals. Their impersonal nature promotes higher stress levels and takes a little bit of humanity out of all of us. Dressing them up a little bit will help keep your staff more human — and that's what your customers want.

KEEP STRESS LEVELS MANAGEABLE

Every job involves a certain amount of stress, no matter how wonderful and easy it may seem to someone on the other side of the cubicle. There is really no such thing as a stress-free job, and those who must deal with customers on a day-to-day basis often are subject to the greatest stress levels of all.

Here are some key tips for keeping stress levels down:

For customer-facing staff:

- **Keep organized.** There's nothing more upsetting than not being able to find a critical piece of paper when you need it. Before you start your work day, spend ten minutes just tidying up your work area, organizing your papers, and planning what needs to be done that day.

- **Take your full lunch break.** Resist the urge to return early "just to finish up some work." It will still be there when you get back. Cutting into your break time may seem like a way to increase your productivity, but in the end, it only creates more stress and is a major cause of burn-out.

- **Avoid getting caught up in office politics and gossip.**

- **In between tasks, stand up, walk around the office, and stretch your legs.**

For managers:

- **High-stress jobs should have reasonable cut-off times.** Overtime is sometimes a necessary reality, but don't expect someone in a high-stress customer-facing position to consistently work late and on weekends.

- **Recognize that customer service is a profession, not a dead-end job.** Customer service agents should be treated as professionals. If not, your employee churn will be high, and your customers will know the difference.

- **Don't expect employees to sacrifice breaks or lunch**

hours. Doing so will create resentment, increase stress, and is illegal, to boot.

KEEPING THEM MOTIVATED

It's hard to keep employees in a high-stress environment motivated. An unmotivated customer service agent is one who will not service your customers like they need to be serviced. "Hands-off" management styles have their place, and it may work well in the IT department, where staff members work best unhindered by management oversight, but in customer service, a certain amount of hand-holding is required.

In fact, dealing with customers every day, eight hours a day, is stressful, simply because of the need to be constantly "on." Customer-facing employees have to always seem friendly and accommodating, no matter how they feel inside. They may have argued with their spouse, got cut off on the freeway on the way to work, spilled coffee on their lap in the morning, and got yelled at by a co-worker, but they still have to smile and create a pleasant interaction for customers — and that's hard to do.

That's why a good customer service manager will always be looking for ways to motivate employees. More money is always at the top of every employee's list, and as we've noted elsewhere in this book, customer service staff should be paid as professionals. However, money is not the only motivator. People walk out on high-paying jobs every day because they can't cope.

The most basic level of motivation comes from when employees are engaged by the company. That is, when the employees have been made to feel like part of the company, rather than just an employee that management does not care about. This is part of a longer process, discussed earlier, that involves bringing the employees "in" to the company — getting them involved in decision-making processes, celebrating victories with them, and keeping them informed about the progress and activities of the entire company outside of the customer service department.

External motivators are a little easier. Besides cold, hard cash in terms of raises and bonuses, external motivators can also take the form of small tokens of appreciation. Something like a company lunch and a little verbal praise will go a long way. Here are some examples of good motivators:

- **Performance rewards.** Specific goals for the department and for individuals should always be a part of motivation. Set goals that are both short term and long term, and celebrate them when they have been achieved. Awards, bonuses, and other goodies like movie passes and gift certificates can be given in response to meeting these goals. Keep in mind, too, that besides the awards themselves, the granting of the awards in a public meeting is also reward in itself. Hold a monthly employee staff meeting where awards are given out and individuals are recognized for superior performance.

- **On-the-spot surprise rewards.** Again, it doesn't have to be a big thing — a pair of movie passes, a box of candy, or some other small thing the employee can enjoy. Here's an example of when these can be given out: A supervisor witnesses an employee handling an exceptionally difficult customer with grace and tact, resolving a major problem and even getting an additional order, a basic "attaboy" is okay, but an "attaboy" along with some movie passes is even better.

- **When you do give verbal praise to an employee, be specific.** Just saying "good job" may sound nice, but it really doesn't say anything specific. It doesn't give feedback to the employee. Saying "good job on handling that difficult customer," on the other hand, praises the employee for a specific action.

Never underestimate the power of recognition and praise. Even without monetary compensation and extra goodies, these two things go a long way. Some managers take the attitude that they expect their staff to consistently deliver good service. That attitude will not reward a good employee, but will punish a bad one, and the result is often devastating to the department and the company — and ultimately causes high turnover and disservices customers.

The "negative reinforcement" school of management does the following:

- Sets very high standards for all workers.

- Does not reward employees who meet or exceed those standards.

- Punishes those who do not meet standards.

It's easy to see that this type of management will quickly fail because there is only negative reinforcement and no positive reinforcement. The employee has no motivation outside of the weekly paycheck to do a good job. Even if the employee is paid well, this type of management will still result in high turnover and unhappy employees and, ultimately, less productive ones. Pay them well, but don't focus on the paycheck as the only source of motivation.

NO BOSS'S PET

One thing that promotes negative office politics is the existence of a "boss's pet." This is the favorite employee, the one who gets all the praise and rewards, and the one who gets singled out all the time. There's a balance to be achieved — as discussed in the previous section, a good customer service manager will provide plenty of praise and rewards to his or her staff. But, one should avoid heaping all the praise on a single individual.

The traditional "employee of the month" contest is sometimes discouraged for this very reason. It is a reward system that only rewards a single employee. Instead of an employee of the month, create an "excellent service award" that is granted at your monthly meetings. This type of award doesn't have to be exclusive; it doesn't have to be given to only a single person. It merely recognizes superior and outstanding work without attempting to single out one person who is the favorite.

Rewarding just one single person a month takes away from other performers. It's important to try to find something to praise in the workers who aren't at the top of the customer service heap but still perform well — doing so will raise their self-esteem, and give them additional motivation to improve.

RESULTS ARE WHAT COUNTS

There are policies, and then there are results. A company creates policies and procedures in order to achieve results, but often a manager or even an entire department will lose sight of the fact that results can come in different packages and through different avenues.

Customer-facing departments and organizations often get bogged down in procedures. True enough, those procedures were created with good intention and often work very well, but over time, a few things inevitably happen:

- **Procedures become out of date.** Employees continue to follow these procedures simply out of habit, because "that's the way we've always done it," or simply because it is required.

- **Innovation is stifled.** Employees resist trying new things that may work better because of the strict focus on procedures.

- **Motivation is lost.** Since the employees have no leeway and no creativity in their job, they become mere functionaries, executing a series of routine tasks that never vary.

- **Customers are disserviced.** In many cases, deviation from policy or "bending the rules" may become necessary to service a particular client in an unusual situation. Unbending adherence to rules and procedures prevent customers from being serviced in these circumstances.

Reward innovation. Departure from procedures and suggestions for new techniques should always be welcome from anyone. Empower customer-facing employees to make decisions and think for themselves. Rules and procedures are necessary, but the very first rule must always be to serve the customer. All other rules are designed to enhance that one.

CREATING AN UNMOTIVATED EMPLOYEE

In addition to creating a motivated workforce, a good customer service manager must also be careful to avoid un-motivating employees.

One example of how to create an unmotivated employee very quickly is to overlook one positive in favor of another. Here's an example: The fast-food business is focused on "fast." Speed is of the essence, and every process is counted in seconds. How fast a sandwich is made, how many seconds a customer waits in line, and how long between the order and the food delivery are all carefully measured and tracked. The very nature of the business requires such a focus.

A particular fast-food restaurant has two employees. Employee "A" is very quick at producing sandwiches, consistently exceeding the time limit that management has imposed. Sandwiches must be created in less than 60 seconds; the first employee always does it in about 30. This employee gets all the praise and extra goodies. Employee "B" meets the 60-second guideline but doesn't usually exceed it. As a result, "B" doesn't usually get much attention. However, a closer look at the situation will reveal that the sandwiches prepared by "A" are adequate, but sometimes a little sloppy. A bit of mayonnaise appears outside the bun, the tomato is off-center, or there are one too many pickles. Sandwiches made by "A" are adequate, but not outstanding. There's nothing egregiously wrong with them and customers don't usually complain about such small things, but still, they don't always look just right. "B," however, always makes the perfect sandwich, with everything exactly in place, neatly prepared and properly wrapped. If a bun comes across with too few sesame seeds or a little spot that has been toasted too much, he will discard it and select another one.

However, over time, since "A" always gets the extra rewards and praise, "B" eventually gets disgusted and either becomes sloppy in order to meet the higher standard or quits entirely. "B" has become unmotivated. The proper way to handle the situation is to continue giving the praise and rewards to "A" for speed, but to also give praise and reward to "B" for perfection and neatness. Besides the weekly award for fastest speed, the manager should also give a weekly "most perfect burger" award.

Other factors in creating an unmotivated employee include:

- **Not explaining the "why" behind procedures.** Policies and procedures may seem like complete nonsense to some employees because they have not been given the "big picture." They have no idea why they have to do a certain task or service the customer in a particular way. An employee has little motivation to carry out a task that has not been properly explained.

- **Keeping employees uninformed.** A customer service

staff that doesn't know what is going on in the company outside their department is going to be a staff that is unmotivated and incapable of doing their job to the best of their ability. Customer service is a doorway — customers' first contact is often here, and your staff must represent not just the customer service department, but the entire company.

- **Inaccessible or distant management.** Managers who distance themselves from the staff create an unmotivated environment, because employees come to feel like they are not part of the company and are not able to approach management with concerns.

A FUN WORKPLACE

During the dotcom era, companies started a new trend: making the workplace a fun place to be. Staff at those early dotcoms were often expected to work long hours, which isn't anything new to corporate life, but the young and innovative entrepreneurs who were behind the dotcom movement did something nobody else had ever done before. They made it fun. They made the workplace a little bit more like home. Many companies took the step of even bringing in recreation rooms, with things like game tables, workout and exercise equipment, Olympic-sized pools, and social areas. One prominent computer company in the Silicon Valley area had a very large decorative garden and walking path, surrounded by flowers and a beautiful fountain. The new dotcom approach changed the entire nature of the employee break room.

Traditionally, an employee break room is a depressing place with little to offer. It contains some tables and chairs, vending machines and a big coffee pot, some posters about minimum wage the government says you have to display, and a phone so you can be called back to your desk. While this gives employees a place to drink their coffee, it gives them little else. A break room, and indeed the entire atmosphere and design of the office, should not be created to look so "institutional." Lacking any of the touches of home, and lacking anything to help the employees relieve stress, staff quickly get bored with their jobs, stressed out, and unmotivated.

On the other hand, an office with a few of these niceties and conveniences creates a whole different atmosphere. One big result is that office politics that results from conflicts diminishes. When employees can go to the company's gym and play racquetball before their shift starts, they gain several benefits: they socialize with each other more, they "blow off steam," and they actually look forward to coming to work every day.

WHAT IS A "POOR ATTITUDE," ANYWAY?

Managers conducting performance reviews are sometimes fond of the phrases "bad attitude" and "not a team player." These terms are vague and meaningless and usually indicative of a deeper problem that the manager is not seeing.

It's up to the manager to dig deeper. More often than not, that "attitude problem" or "team player problem" will turn out to be something else, such as a problem with knowledge or skills. Simply placing customer service reps at a desk and telling them to go to work will often result in this problem—and it's not the employee's fault; it's the manager's for not providing adequate orientation and training. The problem can usually be fixed with some training or instruction.

PERFORMANCE REVIEWS

Office politics, internal squabbles, disputes, and other problems often come from a lack of understanding and direction. Avoiding these problems from the beginning is important, and one way to do that is with the regular performance review. This helps the entire office political scene in two ways:

1. **It helps the managers better understand the employees, what they need, and where they are career-wise.** It helps managers see small problems before they become big ones and gives them a chance to target areas for improvement.

2. **Regular reviews give employees an opportunity to receive and give feedback.** Many problems exist with the chief perpetrators of the problem blissfully unaware that they are creating disturbances! And what's more, too often employees don't have an opportunity to say what's on their mind. The performance review affords that opportunity.

However, the performance review must go beyond being a simple annual function governed by a checklist. Let's take the basic annual performance review, the standard often used in corporate America, as an example. Once a year, the employee trudges into the boss's office. Employee receives a pat on the back and an "attaboy," asked a few generic questions about career goals, and receives the standard 2 percent raise. Nothing really has been accomplished. In fact, because it's only once a year, almost all of the issues, problems, and wins the employee has encountered during the year have passed by and been forgotten.

Instead, the manager should take time to carefully review the time since the previous review — not drawing on memory, but instead reviewing a written performance record that highlights all the wins, successes, failures, and shortcomings that happened throughout the year. Keeping such a record should be an ongoing process.

Besides using the performance log to make sure the entire year's activity is being reviewed properly, managers should focus a bit less on the annual review and a bit more on continuous review. Immediate feedback is often appropriate and more rewarding, as opposed to waiting until the review at the end of the year.

The review is a great opportunity to go beyond simply updating the personnel record. It's an opportunity for managers to keep in touch with their employees, stay on top of problems they may not be aware of, and stop problems before they occur. In addition to the standard review function, a manager should take the performance review as an opportunity to:

- **Learn whether the employee has a complete understanding of his or her job.** The review is a good chance to find places where additional training may be needed. An employee may indeed be performing poorly, but it may well be because nobody ever bothered to provide any training when new software was brought in or new procedures installed.

- **Learn whether the employee has a complete understanding of the company.** The review is an opportunity to discuss with the employee broader issues that go beyond the individual department, and how his or her job relates to the company as a whole.

- **Gain a greater understanding of the "front lines."** The performance review can be educational for the manager as well. It's a time when managers can discuss the day-to-day business processes with each employee on a one-on-one basis—not just to find out if the employee is doing his or her job, but to find out more about what that job entails and whether it can be improved. Very often the employee can bring in new and fresh ideas on how to do things better. The wise manager is the one who listens to that sort of feedback and takes action on it.

An innovative twist here can bring further insight and avoid office politics and other problems. The so-called 360 degree review is something that is done in addition to the standard performance review. Usually, only one person goes through the 360-degree review at a time, and everybody in the department is involved. All of the employee's peers, as well as their bosses and underlings, fill out an anonymous questionnaire regarding the individual, rating him or her in different areas and making narrative comments. Responses are calculated and comments are compiled. This procedure often results in a far greater understanding of not just the employee's strengths and weaknesses, but also the nature of interpersonal relationships in the office, the dynamics that are involved in how your staff works together, and the degree of understanding that exists.

INTERNAL PUBLIC RELATIONS

Public relations shouldn't just be limited to a separate department that creates press releases and places mentions of the company in the media. Public relations is the art of feel-good and spin, but in addition to making your company look good to outsiders, public relations' techniques can also be applied internally to avoid office politics, keep staff members informed, and improve morale.

One of the most basic tools of internal public relations is the company newsletter. Besides publishing relevant HR details, the newsletter is also a good way to share- information from other departments and highlight some employee contributions and successes throughout the company. We've discussed the need for customer service personnel to become informed about the company as a whole; the newsletter is an excellent tool to promote this level of knowledge. This sort of internal communication frequently does not get the attention and respect it deserves. The company newsletter should be an important part of your internal PR strategy.

In between issues of the newsletter, company-wide memos can also serve a useful purpose. If some major noteworthy event occurs—the company gets a major client or a major milestone is reached, or on the other side of the spectrum, a milestone is missed or the company loses a major client, this information should go out in the form of a memo. If the news is positive, names should be mentioned. Instead of saying, "We signed Mega Corporation today for a $10 million contract," say "Jill Smith signed Mega Corporation for a $10 million contract today."

Keep in mind that these internal communications should go out to all employees in all departments—not just some. Don't limit the memos and newsletters to managers or single departments. It may not be immediately obvious why every file clerk in every department should see these things, but in the end, the results will be amazing. Those file clerks will be more knowledgeable about the company, more excited, more motivated, and more likely to do a better job and advance within the ranks of the company. And in customer service especially, the customer service staff who are given these communications on a regular basis will have more direct, usable information that they can use. Customer service people, besides knowing about the product and the customer, should know more general information about the company as a whole.

CHAPTER

14

EFFECTIVE PROBLEM SOLVING

C ustomer service people often wear the hat of the first-line troubleshooter. Determining the customers' needs isn't always as easy as it sounds. When customers have a problem, who want someone to fix it. The customer service person must take responsibility for the fix, even if he or she is not handling it directly.

GETTING INFORMATION FROM YOUR CLIENT

Much problem solving simply is done by asking questions. Sometimes when clients call in with a problem, it's hard for them to describe it. They may be unfamiliar with some of the technology or product names; they just know it's not working right. It's up to the agent to ask the right questions to determine the nature of the problem, and at the same time, not make the caller feel like an idiot for not knowing what to ask for.

Being able to ask the right questions requires the agent to have two types of knowledge:

1. Knowledge about the customer.

2. Knowledge about the product or service.

That's why it's always best to delegate among clients to individual agents so that agents can get to know their callers. Agents are more likely to be able to resolve a problem if they are already familiar with the clients, what products they use, and what types of problems they have had in the past. Even if the agents do not recall that information, giving them immediate access to a client database and call log will go a long way in giving them a good overview of what to expect.

And while to most people it may seem like a no-brainer to require agents to have a good understanding of the company's products and services, it's not always the case. Companies that don't put priority on the call center sometimes just put in low-paid, un-trained workers in the call center, give them scripts and a problem-resolution tree, and expect them to function. The call center employees should be considered professionals, given responsibility and decision-making authority, and access to as much information as they need. They should be trained and knowledgeable about your company's products and services, as well as trained in customer service techniques. Especially in an environment where your product is technical or highly mechanical and requires some skill to manage, call center employees may even need to be degreed, or at least certified in the technology you sell. This does, of course, mean paying them accordingly. When the call center staff is the lowest-paid department in the company, your customer service will suffer.

BE HONEST WITH YOUR CLIENT

The natural tendency of a call center agent is to want to please the client. This is a good tendency, of course, but in our zeal to please clients, we sometimes are afraid to say no.

Sometimes clients make requests that require a little flexibility, and it's always good to try to accommodate whenever possible. Clients will inevitably request something out of the ordinary, something that requires policy to be "bent" a little, or something that requires a little extra effort on your part. You will get loyal customers by empowering your agents to fulfill these little requests whenever possible. But there will be times when the client makes a request that is completely unreasonable, and simply cannot be done. Your equipment can't handle it, you would lose too much money on the deal, or maybe the request is simply technologically impossible. Since we resist saying no to a customer, sometimes agents say something vague, like:

- "Let me see what I can do about that."

- "Let me ask around."

- "I'll have to get back to you on that."

- "I'll put that on my list."

Or worse yet, saying "Sure, we'll take care of that," and then forgetting about it.

In reality, although we want to please customers and accommodate them whenever possible, the customer is not, in fact, always right. When we have to say no, just come out and say it. Do so politely, and offer an alternative if possible, but don't make a promise that can't be kept or imply that something might be possible when it's not.

If a client makes such a request, follow these steps:

1. **Be absolutely certain that the request cannot be filled.** If you are not certain, tell the client you are not sure if the request can be filled, but you will find out if it can be done, and then get back to the client as soon as possible.

2. **If the answer is no, tell the client, politely, and explain why:** "I'm sorry, Mr. Smith, I talked with the guys in engineering; we can't do that for you because our equipment cannot be tooled to make that part."

3. **Offer an alternative solution.**

STOP AND LISTEN

One of the most important things a client service rep can learn is how to listen. Surprisingly, it's a skill that is possessed by fewer people than you might realize. There is a natural tendency, when confronted with a problem, to go immediately into a defensive mode, cut the customer off short, and respond with something like:

- **"I wasn't responsible for that; it must have been the new guy in the office."** This is pushing blame onto somebody else and is nothing but a cop-out and a disservice to the customer. Customers, in fact, don't care who was responsible for it or whether or not you were involved in the initial screw-up. They just want the problem fixed. Regardless of who did it, the agent on the phone must take responsibility for making it right without getting into office politics and the blame game.

- **"We did what we said we would do."** A common way of avoiding responsibility. Customers may call to complain when they receive something late, somebody was rude to them, or they just didn't like what they ordered. Be prepared to apologize for any slight the customers felt, whether it was perceived or real, and be flexible enough to allow them to change an order, even if you did send them what they asked for.

- **"I can't do anything about that."** The worst response of all. This response begs the question "If you can't do anything about that, why are you talking to me?" If an agent's only response is "I can't do anything about that," then there's something wrong: either the agents are not sufficiently empowered by management to take action to remedy the situation, or they are simply not interested in fixing the problem because it is difficult.

The first thing to do when talking to customers is to hear them out. Don't cut them off, even if it seems like they are rambling a bit to you. Listen for key points and take notes while customers are speaking. Respond from time to time with a short affirmation, such as "Yes, I see," or "I understand," but keep the initial responses short while they are talking. The customers must feel that they have your undivided attention and not get the sense that you are just trying to get them off the phone as quickly as possible.

After the customer has presented the problem, here's what you do:

1. Summarize the problem or situation in a few short sentences, and ask the customer, "Is that right?"

2. If there has been a disservice, apologize, regardless of who was at fault.

3. If you are able to remedy the situation immediately, then offer a solution or a choice of solutions right away.

4. Follow up within a few days to make sure the customer is satisfied with your solution.

If, however, you are not able to offer an immediate solution, explain what your course of action will be: "I'm going to present this to my supervisor and come up with a solution." Then, provide a timetable: "I'll get back to you before the end of the day."

BE THE EXPERT

When customers have a problem or a question, they may not be completely familiar with your product or how it should be used. They may not be in a position to understand the best options for themselves, and so they look to you, the customer service agent, to help them out. In situations like this, you need to be more than just a voice on the phone. They're calling you, which means they're calling the company, because they feel that they will be able to get some expert advice and guidance. The words "I don't know" shouldn't be in your vocabulary. Even if you don't know, never say it. Instead, say something like:

- "Let me find that out for you."

- "The team over in (engineering/sales/design/whatever department) will know that. I'll talk it over with them and get right back to you."

- "I'll do some research on that and call you back first thing in the morning."

And when you do make a recommendation, explain your reasoning behind it. Customers want to be informed; they don't just want you to make decisions for them. If, for example, you are recommending that a product be configured a certain way, explain why that configuration will work best, what that configuration will cause the product to do, and what will happen if that configuration is not done.

Whenever possible, give educated options. List the positives and negatives of each of your recommendations, tell the customer what you recommend, but then allow the customer to make the final decision.

TAKE AWAY THE "IDIOT FACTOR"

Sometimes a problem is so simple, it's embarrassing, but it happens. Customers may be unfamiliar with the product or just overworked or distracted to the point where they can't see something that should be obvious. If customers call in to say that a product isn't working right, your procedure is probably to go through the simple solutions first to eliminate the obvious.

You say, "Check the back of the device to make sure the plug is attached to the port."

It's simple and obvious, and probably something most people would already think of before calling tech support, but nonetheless, you ask the question. The customers then look on the back of the device, and sure enough, the cord is hanging loose. They feel stupid for making a call for such a small thing. They might say something like, "Oh my God, you're right; the cord's not plugged in. Gosh, I feel dumb."

At that point, you need to reassure them. Say something like:

- "That's a very common mistake."

- "Oh, it's all right. That happens all the time."

- "Oh, don't worry, the same thing happened to me just last week."

UNDERSTAND WHAT THE CUSTOMER WANTS

It's not always easy to understand just what the customers want when they're in need of customer service, and sometimes what they say they want isn't really what they need.

The first step in understanding the customer's needs is careful recordkeeping and being able to make an immediate review of the customer's history. Having customer records easily accessible, whether it's through an on-screen pop or a filing cabinet next to your phone, will help you to know whether the customer had a similar situation previously and how it was resolved in the past. Gaining a good understanding of previous problems and concerns will help in resolving current issues. Do your homework before trying to offer assistance.

Once you know a bit about the customer's history, listen to what they have to say about their situation, with as little interruption as possible. Once they have explained it, ask relevant questions to draw out the details you need to solve the problem.

Part of understanding what customers want is listening to what they say, but another part is listening to what they're not saying. The customer may want something but may be afraid to say it or may not be knowledgeable enough to communicate that need to you. It's up to you to draw that information out of customers and understand what's going on inside their mind.

BEING THE BEARER OF BAD NEWS

Ever since ancient times, when the king would have the bearer of bad news killed swiftly with a sword, nobody likes to be the one to deliver bad news. It's just part of our natural tendency as human beings. Although reactions hopefully won't be quite so extreme in today's business world as they were in kingdoms of old, customers can still have negative reactions, such as:

- **Anger.** A customer who receives bad news may get angry, and that anger will be directed at the person who delivers the news, regardless of whether or not it was that person's fault directly.

- **Offensive behavior.** Sometimes anger can get out of control, and a customer may cross the line and exhibit behavior that is downright uncivilized, which may include bad language or insults.

- **Threatening behavior.** A customer being told bad news may make threats, ranging from legal action to physical violence.

- **Taking their business away.**

If you must deliver bad news to a customer, keep it short and simple. Don't beat around the bush; just come out and say it in plain language. Here are a few tips for delivering negative news:

1. **Deliver bad news with something else to take the edge off.** For example, suppose production has been delayed for a project. Instead of just saying, "We can't get you your shipment until next Tuesday," say, "We can't get you your shipment until next Tuesday, but the moment it's ready, I will deliver it to you personally the same day, instead of routing it through our shipping department."

2. **Take responsibility for the situation.** Regardless of whom, if anyone, may have been at fault, you are the one who the customers are talking to, and they want you to take care of it for them. Apologize for the situation, and then tell the customers what you are doing to fix it.

3. **Don't place blame.** Suppose your customer runs a men's shop, but you delivered three cases of pink nighties instead of the business suits he was promised. You could say, "Those nitwits in shipping must have switched boxes," or "It must have been that new guy in production; he's not too bright," or "Sometimes I think the people around here

are a few sandwiches short of a picnic." But that would just discourage the customer and cause him to lose faith in your entire organization. Placing blame on even a single individual will reflect badly on the entire company.

4. **Explain why it happened, and what you have done to make sure it doesn't happen again.** Again, without playing the blame game, explain what happened and why. For example, the men's store got the wrong shipment because a ladies' boutique a few blocks away that you also service has a similar store name. Then, explain what you're going to do to avoid the same confusion in the future; for example, "We've added the descriptive words, 'men's store' to the end of your store name in our database so labels will be more descriptive. That should avoid any mix-ups in the future."

WHEN THE CUSTOMER ASKS FOR TOO MUCH

A customer who has been disserviced in some way will come in to your office or shop, sometimes with a specific resolution in mind. Sometimes that resolution is practical and fair, but sometimes it's not. Let's look at the following scenario:

Your company made a custom-designed product for a customer, according to their specifications. Although your engineers advised against a few specific design elements, the customer insisted that you make it exactly to their spec anyway, which you did. A week later, the product broke down because one of those design elements caused a problem. The customer now comes in with a whole new design, insisting that you re-manufacture a whole new product, to a new set of specs, and at no charge. The cost to you would be substantial, and your production crew is currently engaged in another project and you wouldn't be able to get to it for another two weeks. However, you know something about how the product was engineered, and you realize that taking the product into the shop and just replacing the one faulty element would quickly remedy the problem at little expense to you.

Clearly, the customer wants too much. There are some circumstances when you may wish to go out of your way and fix a problem at your own expense, just to satisfy a good customer who made a mistake. That's called goodwill. Even though the problem was the customer's fault, the customer has been with you a long time, has made you a lot of money, and you want to keep his business, so you go ahead and fix the problem and absorb the loss.

But you can't always do that. In this case, the cost is substantial, and the customer is making what is clearly an unreasonable request. The first thing to do is to remain calm and polite, and don't blame the customer directly for bringing in a faulty design. Reiterate that your engineers recommended against it, but do so with tact, by saying something like, "Our engineers wouldn't recommend a design like this, because this part here causes more stress on the rest of the product and will cause a breakdown, which is what happened." Then explain that you can't comply with the request, but you can offer an alternative. Be the customer's advocate and offer a better solution. "To re-manufacturing the entire product, we would have to bill you for shop time, and I know you've already put a lot of time and money into this. Instead, we can take the product back into the shop and replace this element with something more structurally sound. It will only take an hour or so, and we won't charge you for it. You can be up and running again by the end of today."

AVOIDING THE RUN-AROUND

Have you ever been subject to the run-around? You try to get something resolved, and everyone you talk to just wants to pass the problem on to someone else. Or so it seems. It could be that nobody really understands your problem, or it could mean that you're just asking the wrong person. Good customer service will always have a "point person" who takes responsibility for an entire situation, regardless of whether it originated in his or her area or not. However, it's inevitable that it will sometimes be necessary to hand off a customer to a different person. There's a right way to do this without making the customer feel like they're getting the run-around.

Suppose, for example, that your customer has a complicated billing problem. You, as a customer service agent, are trained to handle most billing situations, but this one is particularly troublesome and complicated and would be addressed better by a particular individual in the billing department who has a better understanding of the complexities involved. You could say, "I'm going to transfer you to the billing department," hit a couple buttons on your phone, and pass the problem on to someone else without any further explanation. In that case, what will happen?

- The customer will feel like he is getting the run-around.

- The customer will have to explain his situation all over again to the person you transfer them to.

- You will cause internal conflict with your co-worker in billing, who will resent you for passing the buck.

- You will take yourself out of the loop. As a result, you won't know what the ultimate resolution is, and you won't be able to help the next time the situation comes up, either.

But instead of just transferring the call, here's what you do to avoid a messy situation:

1. Explain to the customer that Bob in the billing department is very familiar with that situation and you'd like to "bring him in on it." Note the way we position the statement. Instead of handing off the customer, you're bringing someone else into the loop. You're not passing the buck, you're looking for a solution.

2. You keep the customer on the line and conference in Bob. With both parties on the line, you summarize the situation to Bob and say, "Can you help us out on this?"

3. Even though Bob is now handling it, you stay on the line to act as facilitator.

4. When Bob is finished, thank him while the customer is still on the line, and ask the customer if there is anything else you can do for him.

Following these procedures ensures that first, you are not being perceived as a "buck passer"; you are being perceived as a helpful person by your customer, even though you may not know the answer to the problem directly. You know who does know the answer, and that's what counts. You've also avoided internal conflict by staying on the line with Bob, explaining the situation to him, and asking for his help. Following this procedure, you are much more likely to get internal cooperation—and the respect of your co-workers—than if you were to simply transfer the call without explanation.

"Getting the run-around" is when clients perceive that they are being passed from person to person without resolution. By staying in the loop from the beginning, you avoid that perception, and are able to make sure that the clients get serviced.

BE ON THE SAME SIDE AS YOUR CUSTOMER

This one should be obvious, but too often it's overlooked. Customer service staff may come to see a customer service problem/resolution scenario as a confrontation, a battle, or an all-out war. They may see themselves as firefighters, constantly putting out fires that have gotten out of control.

In reality, customer service is none of these things. If the customer senses that you are just trying to win, then you have already lost. In the end, both you/your company and the customer must both be winners. You can only accomplish this by being on the customer's side—by being his advocate as you try to resolve whatever problem or dilemma he is facing. You're not there to win a battle; you're there to help your customer solve a problem. Instead of positioning yourself and the customer as opponents, position yourself and the customer as allies, both united against a common enemy, with that enemy being whatever problem the customer has brought to the table.

The first thing to do to create this type of atmosphere is to offer sympathy. Try comments like these:

- "I understand."

- "I know that must be very frustrating."

- "A similar thing happened to me once."

Be specific whenever possible. For example, if the customer has to fill out extra paperwork and this upsets him, say, "I know these forms can take a while to fill out. For someone like you with such a busy schedule, it's frustrating. I'll help you with them however I can, and once they're completed, we can resolve this issue."

Secondly, use "we" statements. This creates a sense of unity and lets the customer know that you want to work with him to solve the problem. Also, make sure that the customer knows that you understand the problem completely. After the customer has explained the situation to you, summarize it back to him briefly, and ask, "Is that correct?"

Being on the same side also requires you to be civil, polite, and friendly. If you're too business-like and abrupt, customers will not feel engaged. They won't feel like you're trying to help them. Try to find some common ground, and don't be in too much of a hurry.

New Age Studies Universal Center

When you're looking for first-hand knowledge on spiritual awareness, want to investigate what is "out there," and are looking for a place to expand your existence, the New Age Studies Universal Center in Niles, Michigan, is there to start you on your journey. The educational center offers a wide range of classes and workshops, as well as metaphysical supplies and unique gifts for sale.

Rev. Julie Perkins, founder of the Center, says that for her, customer service is all about "providing our customers with a quality of service that will result in them feeling really good about their association with us, and make them want to return as customers again and again." The small center operates primarily on a walk-in basis, and so customer service for Rev. Perkins is something provided individually and personally, rather than through technology. But in those areas where technology counts, the Center is on top of it. Their Web site has a comprehensive list of courses that are available, and the Center has a mailing list to keep customers and students informed about what events are coming up.

The Center does get a lot of e-mail inquiries, and since the Center still has only a dial-up connection, it's difficult to do a lot online. Still a work-in-progress, Rev. Perkins says, "We need to work on improving our response time to e-mails. We will obtain a faster Internet connection so that it won't take so long for pages to load, and thus we won't feel like we're wasting so much time in dealing with e-mails, etc."

Providing something truly unique is also a tremendous service to customers, who are unable to find classes like Feng Shui, Creative Visualization, and Dream Interpretation anywhere else in the region. "We're unique in this region in providing what we do," she adds. "We strive to have small class sizes in order to provide more individual attention to our students, and thus they will have a much better learning and retention rate and really feel better about taking courses with us." And while course size is kept small, the selection is rapidly growing, with 42 new courses added to this year's course catalog.

Special incentives have been incorporated to help serve customers better, and the center has recently added memberships, to give long-term customers special enrollment prices and discounts, as well as invitations to members-only special events. And at the end of every class, students are given a questionnaire for feedback—and if the customer fills out the survey, they receive a discount on store purchases.

Visiting the Center, whether it's for classes, to purchase some incense, or just to talk, is always a mind-opening experience, and Rev. Perkins is always on hand to answer questions and make you feel at home.

CHAPTER 15

BEST PRACTICES

This chapter contains some best practices that have helped companies achieve success in delivering superior customer service.

AVOID VOICE MAIL HELL

In the old days, there was always a receptionist in the front office who greeted walk-in customers and answered the phone. Today, more companies are pinched for money and have eliminated this position in favor of putting in direct lines, using voice mail, automated call processing, and other technology. It does save money, and, if done right, it can even make things more efficient. It can also become your clients' worst nightmare if you let it get out of hand.

Voice mail does carry an advantage over leaving messages with a human—there's no chance of error. You say what you want to say, and it's played back to whoever you wanted to talk to.

Avoid an overly complicated series of voice mails and keypad entries. Some of the worst systems require callers to go through three or four levels, and then enter in extra information as well, such as account numbers, before being able to talk to a live person. Ideally, there should be only one layer, or at most two, before a live person is on the other end of the phone. And while requiring callers to enter in account numbers may seem like a good idea, in reality, this saves very little time, causes customers additional inconvenience, and in most cases the agent asks for the same information again once the call is connected anyway.

"PRESS ONE FOR CUSTOMER SERVICE...."

Those annoying "press one to talk to accounting, press two for customer service," and so on, do serve a purpose. With the absence of a live receptionist, callers must have some way of getting to the correct destination. These automated electronic receptionists route calls to the correct person and typically allow callers to enter in an extension number or go to a directory where they can enter in a person's name with the telephone keypad if they don't know the extension.

Typically, the first announcement allows callers to either enter in an extension number or press a number to be connected with a department. In an ideal world, however, a third option should be allowed: ". . . or press zero for an operator." The fact is no matter how efficient your call routing system is, there will always be callers who don't know who they need to speak to, don't know which department they need, or just simply do not want to go through the routing options. There must be an alternative for these people, or you risk losing customers because of it. The call routing system will take the bulk of the call routing burden off of human operators, but for the handful of callers who insist on talking to the operator, provide this option for them. In many cases, you won't even need a dedicated operator; phone systems allow the operator function to be routed around the office so the task can be delegated to several people.

The best call menu will always include an operator option in every level, allowing callers to cut through unnecessary levels and talk to a live person if they need to.

AUTOMATED RESPONSE

There are times when your customers really do need to talk to a live agent when they call in, but you can make the most of your agents and allow them to spend time on the most important calls, while delegating simple requests to an automated system. Callers will appreciate the opportunity to do things like enter their account number in the telephone keypad to get automatic information such as account balances or product availability. Allowing callers to address basic needs like that through an automatic, non-human system is, in most cases, delivering better customer service than using humans to address these day-to-day requests, simply because it allows customers to receive their information faster. As always, however, allow the customers the option of connecting to a live agent; don't make the automated response system the only option.

USE GUIDELINES, NOT SCRIPTS

Have you ever gotten a call from salespeople who aren't very good, and all they do is read a script to you? You can tell they're just reading from a prepared page, and they haven't got a clue as to what they're talking about. They have been provided with a canned pitch, and three or four canned responses to give when you tell them no. These sorts of salespeople usually aren't very successful.

There are times when the canned pitch has to be deviated from, whether it is in a sales capacity, customer service, or anywhere else. A grocery store, for example, required their baggers to ask every customer, "Would you like some help with that?" after their groceries were bagged. But the store made a critical error by making that mandate universal. A decision was made by the management, and handed down without really consulting the front-line folks who do the actual work, and then every bagger had to make that statement, in those exact words, to every single customer. It seemed like a good idea at the time to the managers, who had never worked the counter, but in reality it was a poor idea. True, some people want help with their groceries, but it didn't make sense to make that statement if customers made a very small purchase and had only one small item in their bag. It's a nice service for a bagger to see an elderly person who may struggle to take out groceries, and then offer to help; it's an insult for a bagger to make the same offer to a young, strapping six-foot-tall football player who has three items in his grocery bag.

So it is with customer service. Agents must be able to use discretion in handling different clients; they must be able to respond appropriately to each different situation. Customers are not all the same. They have different needs. Some want hand-holding, while some want only to ask a single question and then take care of the problem themselves.

ANGRY CLIENTS

Sometimes, despite your best efforts, clients will still get angry. Sometimes their anger may be justified if they have been disserviced; sometimes they're just angry people. Either way, the situation must be handled and the anger diffused.

When clients call or come in with steam coming out of their ears, there is a procedure you can follow to address the situation. You do want to diffuse it as quickly as possible, because shouting and angry clients are very likely to cause other clients to be uncomfortable and perhaps leave. Here are some steps to follow in this situation.

1. **If possible, isolate the angry client from other clients.** Politely say something like, "Let's go into the conference room and discuss this over coffee." Usher them into the room as quickly as possible, get someone to bring in refreshments, and close the door.

2. **Let them blow off steam.** Chances are they have gone over what they want to say several times in their head, and they want to say it. They won't be able to be satisfied until they have said everything that was on their mind. Don't try to cut them off short; listen to everything they have to say. Offer short responses, like "Yes, I see," "I understand," or "that must be very frustrating for you." Don't try to solve the problem while they are still venting their anger and having their say.

3. **After a while, they will run out of steam.** They will have said what they wanted to say and will feel a little better. Then it's time for you to offer an apology and regrets for their difficult situation. Before getting into the details of what you can do to solve the problem, offer some sympathetic remarks. "Yes, that's a terrible situation, and it never should have happened," or "You're absolutely right; it never should have happened that way."

4. **Offer a solution.** The agent handling the angry clients should be one who is knowledgeable about the clients and the product or service they use, and the agent should also be empowered to make a decision on the spot to make it right. Fix the problem, offer an alternative, replace the broken part, or do whatever needs to be done.

5. **Offer some extra compensation for the inconvenience.** It doesn't have to be anything big. It could be an offer of a free upgrade, an extra service, a free meal if you run a restaurant, or something of that nature.

6. **Follow up.** You may not want to talk to those clients again and you're glad the whole episode is over, but after you've fixed the problem, the clients need a little special handling. Follow up with a short phone call or letter, again apologizing for their inconvenience, asking them if your actions solved the problem and if there is anything else you can do for them.

7. **Post-analysis.** Get together with all staff members who are involved. Take a good look at the situation, the problem that arose, why it arose, and how it was fixed.

That way, you can help make sure the problem does not happen again.

TALK ON THE SAME LEVEL AS YOUR CLIENT

When you begin a conversation with clients, try to determine their level of expertise and their familiarity with whatever technology may be involved. Once an agent has been involved in a particular industry for a while, it's easy to fall into a trap where the agent uses a great deal of jargon and technical terms, automatically assuming that everybody else will understand. There's a delicate balance to be achieved here. On one hand, talking down to clients may make it seem like you are treating them like a child, while talking on a purely technical, jargon-filled level may confuse them.

There's no single way to talk to everyone. Laypeople may have some passing familiarity with technology, but may require more detailed explanations of products and functions. Avoid referring to products by short names. If it's a long pipe, call it a long pipe, not an "XJY-15."

HANDLE IT YOURSELF WHEN POSSIBLE, BUT CALL IN THE TROOPS WHEN NEEDED

Each customer-facing employee should be empowered with as much authority as possible to handle situations, make exceptions, and resolve problems. Whenever possible, a single agent should be able to take care of all of a customer's needs without having to stop the call, check with somebody else, and then call back. Do recognize, however, when you need to call in help. There may be situations where a resolution is beyond your capabilities, or somebody else is better equipped to handle the problem. It may be that you as an agent have tried everything you have at your disposal, and the customer is still not happy. Then it's time to escalate the call and hand it off to a supervisor or manager or another agent who may be more familiar with the client's particular problem.

REGULAR UPDATES AND COMMUNICATION

Not all customer problems and requests can be solved or fulfilled immediately. Things may take time, and while customers may realize this, they still need to know that you haven't forgotten them. If a project is going to take several weeks to complete, send your customers a short update every week or two just to let them know you're on schedule.

EXTRA DONUT

Throughout the course of this book, we've referred several times to the word "lagniappe," a word you'll come across visiting French-speaking New Orleans loosely translates to "a little bit extra." The thirteenth donut in your box of a dozen is the lagniappe. What it comes down to is a basic customer service premise that you should go the extra mile, give a little bit extra, and just go above and beyond what is expected.

The concept of lagniappe, by its very nature, isn't part of written policy; it's more of a mindset. It's something that is beyond the standard, beyond the tutorials and handbooks. It's above and beyond the call of duty, and giving something that you don't have to give. It's a frame of mind that you must try to put into every customer-facing employee's head from the very beginning. You'll find that when your service organization operates with this concept in mind, you will have more loyal and satisfied customers.

Airlines aren't particularly well known for making customers comfortable; on the contrary, they are quite well known for packing as many people into smaller and smaller seats as they possibly can. When flying on British Airways between New York and London, however, you'll notice a few little extra niceties that the other airlines either haven't thought of or don't care about. Besides the seats being a bit more comfortable than the competition, British Airways provides a little package in the seat back for every passenger. Besides the headphones, in-flight magazine, and other odds and ends, British Airways thought to include a pair of socks in the package, realizing that some passengers, after flying all night, may wish to put on a fresh pair. We don't know of any other airline that does this. It really shows that they are thinking about their customers.

Think about it: Everybody loves getting a gift, a little something-for-nothing, a pleasant surprise. Even if it's not big, it doesn't matter; the point is the lagniappe just shows the customers that you're thinking about them.

"FEEL LIKE A NUMBER"

Make sure that your customers don't just "feel like a number" when they call. There are two ways to approach this; first, by addressing them by name, and second, by providing your own name. Some government agencies sign correspondence with simply an agent number. Imagine how you would feel getting a letter and reading a sentence like this:

- "Please complete the enclosed form and mail back to the attention of Agent #12345 at the above address."

Thankfully, most businesses will at least place a name on correspondence. Nobody wants to talk to "Agent #12345." From the very beginning, this sets up an impersonal environment, from the time the customer calls in, gets the operator, and makes that very strange request: "Yes, hi, I'd like to speak to #12345, please." A customer will resist making such a call. Make sure your agents give their name, address the customer by name, and to the extent possible, handle the same clients on a consistent basis so that a relationship can be established.

MORE ACTION, LESS TALK

Managers sometimes believe that they are promoting good customer service practices when they open up their business catalog and order posters that read, "The customer is always right," and "Service is our number-one priority." Said posters get placed in the employee break room and other areas throughout the company.

These posters do very little to promote customer service. For employees, a poster with a slogan on the wall is not a good motivator—it's just part of the office décor. For customers who see such signs, the posters also do very little. For customers, seeing is believing. Actually delivering good service will go a lot further than putting up a poster that says how much you believe in it.

Customer service must be visible. And by "visible," that doesn't mean putting posters on the wall. It means producing results. A customer who walks into a shop and sees a poster about service isn't really going to give it much thought. They won't go to their friends and neighbors and say, "You should spend your money at that shop. They have a poster on the wall that says they have great service." But poster or not, when they actually receive superior service, they will make the recommendation.

KEEPING UP APPEARANCES

Customer service is 90 percent action and 10 percent appearance. While action is vitally important—customers want to see results—what you, your employees, your office and your building look like will also make a big impact toward how your customers perceive your company.

Regardless of how good your service people are and how well you have trained them, if customers walk into your shop and there is dirt and papers on the floor, the paint on the walls is faded, and your waiting room smells like stale cigarette smoke, the customers will have a perception of how their service will be before you have a chance to deliver it. A poor appearance will create an advanced perception of poor service. Whether service is actually poor or not is besides the point; customers who go in with that expectation are more likely to either walk away before being served or be harder to please from the beginning.

A big tax company in San Francisco had headquarters in one of the city's poorest districts. Vagrants hung around the streets and near the building; the building itself was in poor repair, and very little attention was paid to the furnishings inside. Desks were old. The conference room where clients were brought in was little more than a few large folding tables and chairs, and coffee was served to visiting customers in styrofoam cups. There was no company dress code. When a customer came in from out of town, the Vice President of Sales would have his secretary pick up the customer in the secretary's personal car, a second-hand Ford that usually had used coffee cups and fast food wrappers in the back seat. The company was on the edge of bankruptcy. Customers did get good service, but getting the customers in the first place was becoming harder and harder.

When the company was bought out, the new owner came to town and arrived in his limousine and was appalled at what he saw. Within months, the office was relocated to a skyscraper in the heart of the financial district overlooking San Francisco Bay. Very quickly, there were a lot of changes being made throughout the company. Creating a good appearance became high priority. New measures included:

- New furniture throughout the office, including attractive desks and a long, polished conference table in the conference room. The front waiting room was decorated tastefully with elegant furniture, sofas, and tables that made it look more like a parlor in a mansion than a company waiting room.

- When people waited in the front room to see an agent, they were served coffee or tea in a china cup.

- A company dress code was enforced uniformly, applying

to every employee, all the way down to the file clerks, who now wore suits and ties.

- Original artwork and sculptures graced the common areas, foyer, and conference rooms.

- A professional chauffeur was brought on board, and out-of-town customers were picked up at the airport in a stretch limousine.

The results were astounding. Sales increased dramatically. Employees became more motivated, and clients were happier.

You may not have the budget for a stretch limousine, but you can pay attention to appearance in terms of professional dress, cleanliness of your automobiles, and by adding a few nice touches to the office. A nice set of china cups and a few pieces of artwork don't really cost that much, but it really says to the customer that you are a first-class operation.

THE TEN COMMANDMENTS OF CUSTOMER SERVICE

In closing, we'll leave you with two sets of rules to live by; one for managers and one for customer-facing employees. There are, of course, many more than ten rules; if there's one thing we've tried to impart during the course of this book, it's that customer service isn't always easy. It can't be summarized in a set of platitudes or easy sayings, and there's a lot more to it than putting up a poster that reads "Service is our top priority." Customer service involves technology, it involves a new mindset on the part of both management and staff, and it involves continuous process improvement.

Ten Commandments of Customer Service for Managers

1. **Engage your staff.** That means keep them informed about the broader operations of the company, and make sure that they feel like part of the team.

2. **Avoid data silos.** Make sure all customer-facing information is integrated, and everybody who needs it has access to it—regardless of departmental fiefdoms and internal politics.

3. **Reward your staff.** The paycheck alone isn't enough— motivate them with extras, rewards, praise and accolades, and an occasional free pass to the movies.

4. **Empower your staff.** Give them the tools they need to do the job and the discretion and authority to take care of your customers when situations arise.

5. **Use the best technology.** Customer relationship management technology by itself won't deliver good customer service, but like anything else, it's a tool that your customer-facing employees can use to their advantage and to the advantage of your customers.

6. **Professionalize your customer service staff, don't marginalize them.** Your customer service agents are professionals and should be trained, treated, and paid as such.

7. **Keep multiple channels open to your customers.** Make sure they can contact you through e-mail, phone, fax, IM, and other methods, and make sure that responses are

equal regardless of how contact was made.

8. **Keep training in mind when hiring and maintaining your customer service staff.** Many companies require a college degree, or at least a customer service-specific certification. Additional training may be necessary as well if your product is technical in nature.

9. **Provide de-stressers in the workplace.** Customer service can be a pressure cooker: Make sure that your workplace has some avenue for your people to blow off steam.

10. **Gather information from, and about, your customers.** Take customer surveys to find out what they really want and how they have been treated.

Ten Commandments of Customer Service for Employees

1. **Stick with the problem until you can find a solution.** Don't take the easy way out and say, "We can't do that." Go out of your way to find out how the customer can be served.

2. **Be prepared to offer alternatives.** If your customer makes a request that can't be filled, don't stop the call with "I can't do that." Find something that you can do that will satisfy the customer just as well.

3. **Work with others in the company.** You may need to go a little bit out of your way to bring in someone from another department, but remember, you're a representative of the entire company — not just the customer service department.

4. **Always call the customer by name, and give your own name as well.** Try to make the customer service experience memorable and personal for your customer.

5. **Listen to your customer.** Sure, you're busy, but the customer has a problem, has something to say, and needs to be heard. Don't jump the gun. Let customers speak their mind before you try to resolve the issue.

6. **Take time to de-stress.** Take advantage of whatever amenities your employer provides; if there aren't any, at least take a moment to stand up, stretch your legs, and take a deep breath before you go on to the next customer.

7. **Be creative.** Don't use canned scripts; every customer is different, and every situation requires a new approach. Start each new customer service experience like a blank slate.

8. **Be prepared.** Using whatever technology and information is available to you, gather all relevant data about the client, the client's history with the company, and the current situation you're dealing with, before your interface with the client.

9. **Always go the extra mile.** Remember the concept of "lagniappe"; give the client a little more than they bargained for.

10. **Don't be in a hurry.** Of course, you'll have quotas and deadlines, but if your primary focus is getting clients off the phone, they'll know it, and their interaction with you won't be productive.

GLOSSARY

360 Degree Feedback:
A method in which an employee may receive feedback on their own performance from their supervisor and up to eight co-workers, reporting staff members, or customers.

Absence or Absent (Scheduled):
A period of time off from work that is previously planned during a normally scheduled work period.

Absence or Absent (Unscheduled):
A period of time off from work during a normally scheduled work period that has not been planned.

Absenteeism Policy:
A policy that provides guidance within an organization regarding managing an employee's chronic absence from work.

Acquisitions:
The strategy a company uses to enter a new business area and develop it by buying an existing business.

Adaptive Cultures:
The environment within a company where employees, who are innovative, are encouraged, and initiative is awarded by middle and lower-level managers.

Agile Organization:
An organization that is able to adapt quickly to changing circumstances and customer demands.

Attendance Policy:
The expectations and guidelines for employees to report to work as written, distributed, and enforced by an organization.

Background Checking:
The act of looking into a person's employment, security or financial history before offering employment or granting a license.

Barriers to Entry:
The factors that make it expensive for companies to come into an industry.

Behavioral Interview:
An analysis of answers to situational questions that attempts to determine if you have the behavioral characteristics that have been selected as necessary for success in a particular job.

Benchmarking:
The process of measuring the company against the products, practices, and services of some of its most efficient global competitors.

Benefits:
Additions to employees' base salary, such as health insurance, dental insurance, life insurance, disability insurance, a severance package, or tuition assistance.

Bereavement Policy:
The portion of an employment contract that provides for a certain amount of time off from work when an employee's spouse or close family member passes away.

Bonus Plan:
A system of rewards that generally recognizes the performance of a company's key individuals, according to a

specified measure of performance.

Bottom-Up Change:
A gradual process in which the top management in a company consults with several levels of managers in the organization and develops a detailed plan for change with a timetable of events and stages the company will go through.

Brand Loyalty:
The preference of buyers for the products of particular companies.

Broad Differentiator:
A company that produces items for several market niches.

Broadbanding:
A salary structure in which pay ranges are consolidated into broader categories to reduce overlap with other pay ranges.

Bureaucratic Costs:
The expense of operating an organization or an organiza-

tional structure and control system.

Business Process:
The activity of delivering goods and services to customers or promoting high quality or low costs.

Business-Level Strategy:
The strategy that a company chooses to stress as its competitive theme.

Capabilities:
The skills a company has in coordinating its resources efficiently and productively.

Capable Competitors:
Companies that are able to quickly imitate an innovative company.

Cash Flow:
The amount of cash a business receives minus cash that must be distributed for expenses.

Centralization:
A type of hierarchy in an organization in which upper-level

managers have the authority to make the most important decisions.

Clarity of Expectations:
The concept that before, during, and after strategic decisions are made, managers should have a clear understanding of what is expected of them, as well as an idea of any new rules or strategies.

Close Substitutes:
Products or services that meet the same basic needs of consumers.

Coaching:
A method used by managers and supervisors for providing constructive feedback to employees in order to help them continue to perform well, or to identify ways in which they can improve their performance.

Cognitive Biases:
Errors in the methods human decision makers use to process information and reach decisions.

Commission System:
A system of rewards in which employees are paid based on how much they sell.

Company Infrastructure:
A work environment in which all activities take place, including the organizational structure, control systems, and culture.

Competitive Advantage:
A company's ability to perform better than its competitors through innovation, efficiency, customer responsiveness, and/or quality.

Competitive Bidding Strategy:
A method of requesting bids from several suppliers and awarding a short-term contract to the lowest bidder.

Complementary Assets:
Resources that are required to take advantage of an innovation and to successfully gain a

competitive advantage.

Complementors:
Companies that sell products that go along with the enterprise's own products.

Conflict Aftermath:
The long-term effects that emerge in the last stage of the conflict process.

Congruence:
The state in which a company's strategy, structure, and controls work together.

Consolidated Industry:
An industry dominated by a small number of large companies or even, in extreme cases, by one company.

Consumer-Oriented Business Definition:
A statement that specified the goals of a company in three ways: which customer groups are being satisfied, which are being satisfied, and how they are being satisfied.

Core Competency:
The central capability for creation of value in an organization.

Corporate Development:
The act of identifying certain business opportunities that a company should pursue, how it should pursue them, and how it should withdraw from businesses that do not fit its strategic vision.

Corporate Governance:
The strategies used to watch over managers and ensure that the actions they take are consistent with the interests of primary stakeholders.

Corporate Social Responsibility:
The obligation of a company to build certain social criteria into their strategic decision-making.

Corporate-Level Strategy:
A strategy in which the business identifies how they should maximize the long-run

profitability of the organization.

Cost-Leadership Strategy:
A strategy in which a company attempts to outperform competitors by doing everything it can to produce goods or services at a lower cost.

Counseling:
The act of providing daily feedback to employees regarding areas in which their work performance can improve.

Current Ratio:
The ratio of a business' current assets against its current liabilities.

Customer Defection Rate:
The percentage of a company's customers who leave for competitors in the period of a year.

Customer Response Time:
The amount of time for goods to be delivered or services to be performed.

Customer Responsiveness:

The ability of a company to identify and meet its customers' needs.

Customers' Needs:
The desires, wants, or cravings to be satisfied by means of a particular product or service.

Customization:
The act of varying features of a good or service in order to tailor it to the unique needs of individuals or groups of customers.

Cycle:
An iteration of the planning process which begins with the corporate mission statement and major corporate goals.

Debt-to-Assets Ratio:
The ratio of total debt of a company to its total assets. A company is thought to be more financially sound at lower ratios.

Debt-to-Equity Ratio:
The measurement creditors have if the business is forced

to liquidate. The more debt a company has relative to its equity, the higher a risk the company is.

Decentralization:
An organizational hierarchy in which authority has been delegated to divisions, functions, managers, and workers at lower levels in the company.

Decline Stage:
The portion of the industry life cycle in which growth declines for a variety of reasons includ ing technological substitution, demographics, social changes, and competition.

Devil's Advocacy:
A way of improving decision-making by generating a plan and a critical analysis of that plan.

Dialectic Inquiry:
A way to improve decision-making by generating a plan and a counter-plan.

Differentiation:
The method a company uses to allocate people and resources to certain tasks in the organization to create value.

Differentiation Strategy:
A strategy which a company uses to achieve a competitive advantage by creating goods or services that customers perceive to be unique in some important way.

Discipline:
A process of dealing with job-related behavior that does not meet communicated performance expectations.

Distinctive Competency:
The unique ability or strength that enables a company to achieve the best efficiency, quality, innovation, or customer responsiveness to attain a competitive advantage.

Diversification:
The process of entering into new industries or business areas.

Divestiture:
The way in which a company sells the whole business to exit an industry.

Divestment Strategy:
A strategy by which a business makes the most of its net investment recovery from a declining industry by selling it early before it has gone into a steep decline.

Dividend Yield:
The return shareholders receive in the form of dividends.

Division:
The portion of a company that operates in a particular business area.

Downsizing:
The process of reducing the employees headcount in an organization.

Dress Code for Business Casual:
A company's objective to enable employees to project a professional, business-like image while experiencing the advantages of more casual and relaxed clothing.

Economies of Scale:
The cost advantages associated with output from a large company.

Economies of Scope:
The cost advantages achieved by sharing resources such as manufacturing facilities, distribution channels, advertising campaigns, and research & development by two or more business units.

Efficiency:
The measurement derived from dividing output by input.

Embryonic Industry:
An industry that is in the beginning stages of development.

Emergent Strategy:
An unplanned response to unforeseen circumstances.

Emotional Intelligence:

A term that describes a bundle of psychological characteristics that many strong leaders exhibit (self-awareness, self-regulation, motivation, empathy, and social skills).

Empathy:
The psychological characteristic that refers to understanding the feelings and viewpoints of subordinates and taking them into account when making decisions.

Employee Empowerment:
The process of enabling or authorizing an individual to think, behave, take action, and control work and decision-making autonomously.

Employee Involvement:
The act of creating an environment in which people may impact decisions or actions that affect their jobs.

Employee Stock Option Plan (ESOP):
A system of rewarding employees in which they may buy shares in the company at below-market prices.

Employment Eligibility Verification (I-9):
The form required by the Department of Homeland Security U.S. Citizenship and Immigration Services to document an employee's eligibility to be employed in America.

Engagement:
The process of involving individuals in active decision-making by asking them for their input and by allowing them to refute the merits of one another's ideas and assumptions.

Exempt Employee:
Employees who are not confined by the laws governing standard minimum wage and overtime.

Exit Barriers:
Economic, strategic, or emotional factors that prevent

companies from leaving an industry even when returns are low.

Experience Curve:
The regular cost deductions per unit that occur over the life of a product.

External Stakeholders:
All individuals and/or groups outside the internal stakeholders who have a claim on the company.

Factor Conditions:
The quality and cost of production factors.

Factor Endowments:
The position of a nation in factors of production such as skilled labor or infrastructure. One of Porter's four attributes of a nation or state that have an impact on competition between companies around the world.

Family and Medical Leave Act (FMLA):
The legislation which states

that covered companies must grant an eligible employee up to 12 weeks of unpaid leave during any 12-month period of time for one or more of the covered reasons.

Feedback:
The information given to or received from another person regarding the impact of their actions on a person, situation, or activity.

Felt Conflict:
The type of conflict occurring at the stage in which managers start to personalize the disagreement.

Flat Structure:
An organization with few hierarchical levels resulting in a relatively wide span of control.

Focus Strategy:
A company strategy in which the business concentrates on serving the needs of a limited customer segment, defined by geography, type of customer,

or product line segment.

Foreign Operations Department:
The part of an organization used to oversee the international sale of products made domestically.

Fragmented Industry:
An industry which contains a large number of small or medium-sized companies, and none of them are in a viable position to dominate the industry.

Franchising:
A business strategy in which the franchisor grants the franchisee the right to use the parent company's name, reputation, and business skills at a particular location or area.

Free Cash Flow:
The flow of cash that is in excess of what is required for all investment projects once all expenses have been paid.

Garnishment:
A legal procedure in which a person's earnings are withheld by an employer for the repayment of a debt.

General Manager:
A person who bears all responsibility for the organization's overall performance or that of one of its major self-contained divisions.

Generation X:
The generation of people who were born between 1965 and 1976 (or 1980, depending on the source). "Gen Xers," as they have been called, tend to be independent, informal, entrepreneurial, and seek emotional maturity.

Geographic Structure:
An organization in which geographic areas become the basis for grouping organizational activities.

Global Learning:
The process in which the skill

flow and products offered go from the local country to a foreign subsidiary and back again, or from one foreign subsidiary to another.

Global Product Group Structure:
A type of organizational method in which a headquarters for a product group is created for the purpose of coordinating the domestic and foreign activities within that product group.

Global Strategy:
A strategy in which a company tries to increase its profitability by reaping the cost benefits that come from the effects of the experience curve and economies in other locations.

Goal:
The future state a company attempts to reach.

Gross Profit Margin:
A figure signifying the percentage of sales that will be able to cover operating expenses.

Group-Based Bonus System:
A type of reward system in which project teams are rewarded based on group productivity.

Groupthink:
A method of decision-making in which a group of decision-makers embarks on a course of action without questioning potentially hidden assumptions.

Growth Industry:
An industry in which initial demand expands rapidly as many new consumers enter the market.

Growth Strategy:
A business-level investment strategy for a company that has a goal of maintaining a relative competitive position in a rapidly expanding market and possibly increasing it.

Harvest Strategy:
Also called Asset Reduction. A strategy in which a company limits or decreases its investment in a business but takes advantages of the investment as much as possible.

Horizontal Differentiation:
The way in which the company focuses on the grouping of people and tasks into functions and divisions to meet the objectives of the business.

Horizontal Merger:
A joining of two companies that provide similar products or services.

Human Resources:
(1) The people who are part of an organization and its operations. (2) The business function that deals with the employees of a company.

Independent Contractor:
A person or a business that performs services or supplies a product for a person or a business under a written or implied contract.

Industry:
A group of companies that offer products or services that are similar to each other.

Informal Power:
A manager's authority that derives from the company's corporate and business-level strategies, which assigns some functional or divisional managers more authority than others.

Innovation:
Something that is novel or unique in the marketplace.

Intangible Resources:
A nonphysical resource to which a company has access.

Integration:
The process by which a company coordinates people and functions to accomplish certain tasks within the organization.

Intended strategy:
A strategy that has been planned and scoped.

Ivory Tower Planning:
A strategy that treats planning as an exclusive function of top-level management.

Job Offer Letter:
A written document that confirms the details of an offer of employment, including details such as the job description, reporting relationship, salary, bonus potential, and benefits.

Joint Ventures:
A method of entering and developing new business areas which involves establishing a new business in collaboration with a business partner.

Labor-Management Glossary:
A comprehensive list of the definitions of labor management terms provided by the U.S. Office of Personnel Management.

Latent Conflict:
The possible conflict that may flare up when the right sort of conditions occur.

Leadership Strategy:
A strategy in which a company attempts to become the dominant player by picking up the market share of companies as they leave the industry.

Learning Effects:
The cost savings that come from learning while performing the task.

Liquidation:
The process during which a company leaves an industry by selling off its assets.

Liquidity:
A measurement of a company's ability to pay short-term expenses.

Long-Term Contracts:
Also called Strategic Alliances. Long-term cooperative relationships between two or more companies.

Management Buyout (MBO):
The act of selling a business
unit to its management.

Market Concentration Strategy:
A business investment strategy in which the goal for the
company is to specialize in a
particular niche or product in
order to narrow and strength-
en its position.

Market Development:
The approach which compa-
nies take to find new markets
for their products or services.

Market Penetration:
An investment strategy in
which a company concentrates
on market share expansion in
its existing product markets.

Market Segmentation:
The method by which a company decides to group customers based on needs or preferences to gain the competitive
advantage.

Marketing and Sales:
The business activities that are

concentrated around value creation by affecting the percep-
tions of customers, and reporting consumer needs back to
the research & development
division.

Marketing Strategy:
The stand a company takes
regarding pricing, promotion,
advertising, product design,
and distribution.

Mass Customization:
The ability of a company to
use flexible technology for
manufacturing in order to
provide both low cost and
products that meet the needs
of consumers.

Mature Industry:
An industry in which the market is completely saturated,
and demand is limited to that
for replacement.

Millennials:
Current employees who were
born between 1980 and 2000.
The stereotypical millennial

has developed work tendencies from doting parents, a structured life, and more contact with diverse people.

Minimum Efficient Scale:
The minimum size of a production plant necessary to gain significant scale economy.

Minimum Wage:
The minimum amount of compensation per hour for covered, nonexempt employees as defined by the Fair Labor Standards Act (FLSA) and by local states.

Mission Statement:
A brief but precise definition of what an organization does and why.

Motivation:
A psychological portion of emotional intelligence that refers to a passion for work that goes beyond money or status and enables a person to pursue goals with energy and persistence.

Mutual Dependence:
The state of a company relying on an independent supplier for a vital input and the supplier relying on the company as the only possible customer for its specialized output.

Negativity:
The concept and expression of unhappiness, anger, or frustration to other employees in the workplace.

Net Profit Margin:
The percentage of sales profit earned.

Networking:
The act of building interpersonal relationships that could be mutually beneficial.

New Employee Orientation:
Also call Induction. The process of orienting a new employee to a company, usually performed by one or more representatives from the Human Resources department.

New-Venture Division:
An organizational group created with the authorization
to experiment and take risks
without scrutiny of top management.

Niche Strategy:
The approach in which a company concentrates on pockets
of demand that seem to be
stable or are declining more
slowly than the rest of the
industry.

Non-Exempt Employee:
Employees who are protected
by the laws governing standard wages and overtime.

Operating Budget:
A plan stating how managers
intend to use organizational
funds and resources in order
to achieve organizational goals
in the most efficient way
possible.

Operating Responsibility:
The authority to oversee
day-to-day operations which

is held by divisional management in a multidivisional
structure.

Operations Manager:
An individual who is responsible for particular business
operations.

Opportunism:
The act of a strategic partner
stealing technology and/or
market share.

Opportunity:
A condition in the external
environment that a company
may take advantage of in
order to implement strategies
that could earn higher profits.

Optimism:
The ability or tendency to
look at the positive side of a
situation and/or to expect the
best possible results from any
series of events.

Organization Bonus System:
A system of rewards based on
the performance measurement
of the organization during the

most recent time period.

Organizational Conflict:
The struggle that arises when the one organizational group is moving to achieve their goals but blocks the same behavior of another group in the process.

Organizational Culture:
The particular collection of values and norms shared by people in an company which controls the way they interact with each other and with outside stakeholders.

Organizational Design:
A the process of selecting a combination of business structure and control systems that allows a company to pursue its strategy in the most effective way.

Organizational Norms:
The expectations that prescribe the appropriate behavior for employees in certain situations.

Organizational Politics:
The strategies that managers use to obtain and use power in order to influence business processes to further their own interests.

Organizational Socialization:
The method of people internalizing and learning the behavior and values of a culture in order to fit in.

Organizational Values:
Concept regarding the goals that individuals within an organization should pursue and what behavioral standards they should follow to achieve these goals.

Orientation:
See: New Employee Orientation.

Output Control:
A system in which certain managers estimate appropriate goals for each division, department and employee, and measure actual performance in

relation to these goals.

Outsourcing:
The act of paying another individual or business to perform certain internal processes or functions.

Parallel Sourcing Policy:
The business practice of entering into long-term contracts for the same part from two different suppliers.

Perceived Conflict:
Conflict that occurs when managers are made aware of clashes within an organization.

Performance Management:
A policy for dealing with behavior on the job that does not meet expected and communicated performance standards.

Piecework Plan:
A system of rewards in which output can be more accurately measured, and employees are paid based on a set amount for each unit of produced output.

Potential Competitors:
Companies that do not currently compete in an industry but would be able to compete if they choose to do so.

Power:
The capability of an individual, function, or division to cause another to do something it would not have done if left to its own devices.

Power Balance:
A state in which no single business unit influences the whole enterprise.

Price Cutting:
The act of reducing the price of products or services below a standard level in an attempt to reduce competition and lead to increased sales.

Price Leadership:
The assumption of responsibility by one company for setting the pricing in an industry.

Price Signaling:
The strategy in which compa-

nies increase or decrease their product pricing to convey their intentions to other companies, thereby influencing the way competitors price their products.

Product Development:
The creation of new or improved products that will replace older products.

Product Differentiation:
The act of creating a competitive advantage by designing goods or services specifically to satisfy the needs of consumers.

Production:
The act of creating a good or service through a business.

Product-Oriented Business:
A company that concentrates primarily on sold products and the intended markets.

Profit Ratios:
A way of measuring how efficiently a company uses its resources.

Profit Strategy:
A business-level investment strategy in which a company attempts to maximize the current returns from previous investments.

Profit-Sharing System:
A system of rewards that compensates employees based on the company's profit during a specified time period.

Progressive Discipline:
A process for dealing with behavior on the job which does not meet expected and communicated performance standards.

Project Boss:
The figure of authority for a particular project.

Project Management:
The process of applying knowledge, skills, tools and techniques to a wide range of activities in order to meet the requirements of the particular project.

Promotion:
The act of advancing an employee to a position with a higher salary range maximum.

Quality:
A measurement of excellence in the desirable characteristics of a product, a process, or a service.

Randomization:
The act of distributing scheduled start times for various clients within a certain percentage of the schedule's startup window.

Recognition:
A practice of providing attention or favorable notice to another person.

Recruiter:
People who are hired by a company to find and qualify new employees for the organization.

Reduce:
To free up space in the database or the recovery log in order to allow a volume to be deleted. Contrast with: Extend.

Resources:
The inputs available to a company by means of financial, physical, human, technological, or organizational avenues.

Restructuring:
A method of improving company performance by reducing the level of differentiation and downsizing the number of employees to decrease operating expenses.

Return on Investment (ROI):
A measurement of the money that has been gained as a result of certain resource investments.

Screening Interview:
A quick, efficient discussion that is used to qualify candidates before they meet with the hiring authority.

Script:
See: IBM Tivoli Storage Manager Command Script.

Self-Awareness:
The psychological characteristic of a person's emotional intelligence in which he is able to understand his own moods, emotions, drives, and his effect on others.

Self-Discipline:
The psychological ability to control one's own behavior.

Self-Regulation:
The psychological ability to control or redirect one's own disruptive impulses or moods.

Service:
The business activity that concentrates on providing after-sales service and support.

Sexual Harassment:
The act of an employee making continued, unwelcome sexual advances, requests for sexual favors, and/or other verbal or physical conduct of a sexual nature toward another employee against her/his wishes.

Social Skills:
The psychological ability to interact purposefully with others at a friendly level.

Span of Control:
The number of employees a manager manages directly.

Spin-Off:
The act of selling a business unit to outside investors.

Standardization:
The level at which a business defines how decisions are to be made so that the behavior of employees becomes predictable.

Strategic Alliances:
Cooperative agreements between companies that are sometimes also competitors.

Strategic Change:
The movement of a company toward a desired future state to increase its competitive advantage.

SWOT Analysis:

Strengths-Weaknesses-Opportunities-Threats. An examination of these four aspects of a company.

Fair Labor Standards Act (FLSA):
The legislation that requires a company to pay a non-exempt employee who works more than a 40 hour week 150 percent of their regular hourly rate for the overtime hours.

Threats:
Conditions in the environment outside a company that endanger the integrity and/or profitability of its business.

Top-Down Change:
An adjustment that occurs when a strong upper-management team analyzes how to alter strategy and structure, recommends an appropriate course of action, and moves quickly to restructure and implement change in the organization.

Total Quality Management (TQM):
A philosophy of management that concentrates on improving the quality of a company's products and services and stresses that all operations should head toward this goal.

Unemployment Compensation:
A policy created by the Social Security Act of 1935 to protect workers who lost their jobs due to circumstances outside of their own control.

Values:
Traits or characteristics that are considered to be worthwhile and that represent an individual's priorities and driving forces.

Vertical Integration:
A strategy in which a company produces or disposes of its own inputs or outputs.

Virtual Corporations:
Companies that have pursued

strategies involving extensive outsourcing.

Vision:
Also called a Mission. A statement of the goals that the company would like to achieve over the medium- to long-term.

Yuppies:
A slang term referring to young, upwardly mobile, urban professionals who are focused on making money and buying expensive items.

INDEX

BIOGRAPHY

Dan Blacharski has been a professional writer and online entrepreneur for over 15 years. He has written four books and ghost-written several others; has produced thousands of print and online features, articles and columns; and has helped many Internet companies refine their messaging. A refugee from Silicon Valley, Dan was there during the "dotcom boom," witnessing first-hand the incredible rise and fall of countless empires, and gaining insight into what makes a new-era Internet company succeed or fail. He worked directly with many of these companies, helping them to refine their messaging.

Two of Dan's own entrepreneurial dotcom ventures are the Five Buck Boutique (**www.fivebuckboutique.com**), an online same-price store; and We Know The Answers (**www .weknowtheanswers.com**), an advertiser-supported online informational site. He currently lives in South Bend, Indiana, with his lovely wife Charoenkwan; but having never gotten quite used to the frigid midwest, they spend their winters in Bangkok.

DESIGN YOUR OWN EFFECTIVE EMPLOYEE HANDBOOK: HOW TO MAKE THE MOST OF YOUR STAFF WITH COMPANION CD-ROM

If you have employees, you need employment policies in writing distributed to every employee. The U.S. Supreme Court has ruled that businesses can protect themselves against damages and liability against employee lawsuits by providing clear, written policies covering the rights and responsibilities of their employees.

Our Employee Handbook Template is the ideal solution to produce your own handbook in less than an hour. The companion CD-ROM in MS Word contains the template, which you can easily edit for our own purposes; just fill in the blank. The book discusses various options you may have in developing the policies. Our employee handbook has been edited and approved by lawyers specializing in employment law. Developing your own handbook now couldn't be easier or less expensive!

Topics include: equal employment opportunity, age discrimination, Americans with Disabilities Act (ADA), workers or applicants with AIDS, unacceptable job performance, termination, substance abuse, drug and alcohol testing, safety, harassment, compensation policies, job classifications, recordkeeping, overtime, employee performance evaluations, wage and salary reviews, payroll deductions, reduction in wages, pay periods, payroll advances, wage garnishment, severance pay, unemployment compensation, operating policies, ethical standards, open-door policy, smoke-free workplace, dress code, flexible scheduling, telecommuting, absenteeism, tardiness, confidentiality, employee privacy, electronic communication, responsible use of equipment, e-mail and Internet, prohibited content, copyrighted materials, responsible use of cell phones, security procedures, telephone usage, use of company vehicles, solicitation for outside causes, outside employment, personnel files, release of information, access to files, possession of weapons, improper personal conduct, company benefits, time off, holidays, vacations, sick leave policies, bereavement, jury duty, education and training, leaves of absence, Family and Medical Leave Act, personal or medical leaves not required by law, military leave, insurance, on-the-job accidents or injuries, medical/life insurance, flexible benefit plans, pension, and profit sharing.

288 Pages • Item # GEH-02 • $39.95 with Companion CD-ROM

To order call 1-800-814-1132 or visit www.atlantic-pub.com

365 Answers About Human Resources for the Small Business Owner: What Every Manager Needs to Know About Workplace Law

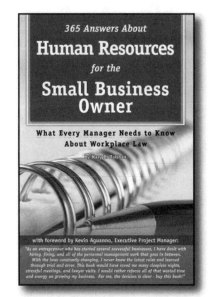

Finally there is a complete and up-to-date resource for the small business owner. Tired of high legal and consulting fees? This new book is your answer! Detailed are over 300 common questions employers have about employees and the law; it's like having an employment attorney on your staff.

Topics include: equal employment opportunity, age discrimination, Americans with Disabilities Act (ADA), workers or applicants with AIDS, unacceptable job performance, termination, substance abuse, drug and alcohol testing, safety, harassment, compensation policies, job classifications, recordkeeping, overtime, employee performance evaluations, wage and salary reviews, payroll deductions, reduction in wages, pay periods, payroll advances, wage garnishment, severance pay, unemployment compensation, operating policies, ethical standards, open-door policy, suggestions and customer feedback, smoke-free workplace, dress code, work schedule, flexible scheduling, telecommuting, absenteeism, tardiness, confidentiality, employee privacy, electronic communication, responsible use of equipment, e-mail and Internet, prohibited content, copyrighted materials, responsible use of cell phones, security procedures, telephone usage, use of company vehicles, solicitation for outside causes, outside employment, personnel files, release of information, access to files, possession of weapons, improper personal conduct, company benefits, time off, holidays, vacations, sick leave policies, bereavement, jury duty, education and training, leaves of absence, Family and Medical Leave Act, personal or medical leaves not required by law, military leave, insurance, on-the-job accidents or injuries, medical/life insurance, flexible benefit plans, pension, and profit sharing.

288 Pages • Item # HRM-02 • $21.95

To order call 1-800-814-1132 or visit www.atlantic-pub.com

How to Hire, Train & Keep the Best Employees for Your Small Business: With Companion CD-ROM

Getting the right people in the right job and then getting them to stay are the key elements in effective business organizations. It sounds straightforward, and many business-people simply put an ad in the paper, wait for the applications to arrive, do some interviewing, and then hire the people they liked the best. Boom, done! Then all hell starts breaking loose: there are attendance problems, attitude problems, and personality conflicts; the business is suffering; the employees are suffering; and management is barely able to keep the ship afloat. What went wrong?

The short answer is they hired the wrong people; they failed to make human resource management a priority. The good news is that careful planning and strategic management of the recruitment, hiring and retention processes will greatly improve success; the bad news is that HR management is not an exact science because people are unpredictable. Fortunately, there are many strategies, techniques and practices proven to improve all aspects of people management.

These are the skills you'll learn in How to Hire, Train & Keep the Best Employees for Your Small Business. This book covers all the essential elements of employee management in an easy-to-understand and practical manner. Topics include:

- Successful Recruitment Strategies—how to find good, potential employees.

- Hiring and Interviewing—asking the right questions, the right way.

- Effective Communication—giving and receiving information effectively.

- Training—improving employee performance.

- Motivation—creating job satisfaction.

- Leadership and Team-Building—influencing employees to work effectively.

The companion CD-ROM contains dozens of employee training and human resource forms including: unique employment applications, interview questions and analysis, reference checks, work schedules, rules to live by, reporting forms, confidentially agreement, and an extensive human resource audit form. Simply print out any form you need, when you need it.

288 Pages • Item # HTK-02 • $29.95

To order call 1-800-814-1132 or visit www.atlantic-pub.com

365 Ways to Motivate and Reward Your Employees Every Day—With Little or No Money

"I LOVE my job!" Is that what your employees are saying? Sadly, according to the U.S. Department of Labor Statistics, American businesses lost an average of 25 days of work in 2001 due to employee anxiety and stress. Don't let your business become part of this dismal statistic. You can improve employee morale and create a harmonious workplace, which will increase profits and productivity.

This new book is packed with hundreds of simple and inexpensive ways to motivate, challenge and reward your employees. Employees today need constant re-enforcement and recognition—and here's how to do it. This is not a "theory" book. You will find real-life, proven examples and case studies from actual companies that you can put to use immediately. You can use this book daily to boost morale, productivity and profits. This is your opportunity to build an organization that people love to work at with these quick, effective, humorous, innovative and simply fun solutions to employee work challenges. Make your business a happy place to work, and reap the benefits. **288 Pages • Item # 365-01 • $24.95**

501+ Great Interview Questions for Employers and the Best Answers for Prospective Employees

For anyone who hires employees, this is a must-have book. It is also essential for anyone searching for a new job or going on a job interview.

Hiring new employees to fill a job vacancy is one of any manager's most important responsibilities. This new book contains a wide variety of carefully worded questions that will help make the employee search easier. These questions can help you determine a candidate's personality type, the type of work he or she is best suited for, and if the person will mesh with your existing employees and workplace. Once you learn the right questions to ask, you'll get the best employees.

As you know, it is not always the best candidate that gets the job—but often the person who interviews the best. For the prospective employee, learn how to sell yourself and get the job you want! From this new book you will learn how to answer the toughest interview questions by being fully prepared and understand what employers are looking for.

288 Pages • Item # 501-02 • $24.95

To order call 1-800-814-1132 or visit www.atlantic-pub.com

2,001 Innovative Ways to Save Your Company Thousands by Reducing Costs: A Complete Guide to Creative Cost Cutting and Boosting Profits

For the small business owner, every dollar you can save by reducing costs goes directly to the bottom line in increased profits. This new book details over 2,000 specific ways that your company can reduce costs today. This is not a "theory" book; there is practical advice on thousands of innovative ways to cut costs in every area of your business. Not only is the idea presented, but the pertinent information is provided such as contact information and Web sites for companies, products, or services recommended.

You will discover over 2,000 practical insider techniques and tips that have been gleaned from successful business operators from around the world and tested in real-life businesses applications. You can put this information in place today to reduce expenses and expand profits. Easy to read and understand, this step-by-step guide will take the mystery out of how to reduce costs in several critical areas: office, operations, labor, cost of goods sold, advertising, marketing, human resources, insurance, employee benefits, compensation, pension plans, training, accounting, software, Web site, mailing, shipping and receiving, rent, interest and debt, utilities, and hundreds more.   **288 Pages • Item # IWS-02 • $21.95**

365 Foolish Mistakes Smart Managers Make Every Day: How and Why to Avoid Them

Here's a very surprising statistic: Within the first 18 months on the job, 40 percent of all management newcomers fail by either getting fired, quitting, or receiving a bad review, according to Manchester Inc., a business consulting group. Some first-timers are overwhelmed by their newfound power while some are weighed down by the responsibility. But for most, the overriding concern is to avoid personal failure.

This new groundbreaking book will guide the new manager to success and avoid the many common mistakes and pitfalls along the way. You will learn how to face the unique challenges every day in your job and offer detailed and innovative solutions to help you achieve your potential. Learn how to become a true leader who commands respect, commitment, and credibility.

288 Pages • Item # FMS-02 • $21.95

To order call 1-800-814-1132 or visit www.atlantic-pub.com